PRAISE FOR

THE VILLAGE CHIEF

A youth coach's impact can reach far beyond sports. Wanting to do it right is not enough. You have to learn how to do it. *The Village Chief* is the perfect place to start. Coach Cleland doesn't just lay out the road map for becoming a great coach, he provides concrete tools to use along the way.

—Ben Watkins
Writer/Producer
Youth Coach

T0125749

Steve Cleland has created a must-read book for anyone who strives to lead. The lessons learned in these pages are vital to achieving success not only on the playing fields but also in the business world and, more importantly, in your personal life.

I went into this expecting another book preaching about "How to coach MY WAY!" but came out of it with a shocking amount of valuable takeaways to utilize in both my business and personal life. From the "gut punch" in the introduction to tying it in a bow with the "little things" at the end, this is a must-read for anyone trying to make a difference in the lives of people you touch.

—Lance Giroux
Executive Vice President in International Sales and Marketing
Former Collegiate Baseball Player (Boston College)
Youth Coach
Youth League President (Little League, ASA Softball)

Steve Cleland perfectly captures what a coach needs to establish an overall game plan to best serve the athletes and parents involved. It's essential to start with clear expectations, realistic goals, and achievable outcomes. Mr. Cleland outlines a simple but effective road map for all coaches to follow.

—Chris Keldorf
Executive Vice President, Fusionetics Sports
Former Quarterback, North Carolina Tar Heels (1996-1997)
Youth Coach

Steve has carried over his strong values as an exceptional student-athlete to the world of youth coaching. His book, *The Village Chief,* should be required reading for all coaches of young athletes, as it entertains every aspect of coaching in a fair and compassionate manner.

—Jeff Attwood
Retired School Teacher
Sports Coach for Forty Years

THE VILLAGE CHIEF

THE
VILLAGE
CHIEF

How to Be the Youth Sports Coach Your
Team Wants ... and Your Village Needs

STEVE CLELAND

Advantage.

Published by Advantage, Charleston, South Carolina.
Member of Advantage Media Group.

ADVANTAGE is a registered trademark, and the Advantage colophon is a trademark of Advantage Media Group, Inc.

Printed in the United States of America.

10 9 8 7 6 5 4 3 2 1

ISBN: 978-1-64225-071-8
LCCN: 2019919725

Cover and layout design by David Taylor.

This publication is designed to provide accurate and authoritative information in regard to the subject matter covered. It is sold with the understanding that the publisher is not engaged in rendering legal, accounting, or other professional services. If legal advice or other expert assistance is required, the services of a competent professional person should be sought.

Advantage Media Group is proud to be a part of the Tree Neutral® program. Tree Neutral offsets the number of trees consumed in the production and printing of this book by taking proactive steps such as planting trees in direct proportion to the number of trees used to print books. To learn more about Tree Neutral, please visit www.treeneutral.com.

Advantage Media Group is a publisher of business, self-improvement, and professional development books and online learning. We help entrepreneurs, business leaders, and professionals share their Stories, Passion, and Knowledge to help others Learn & Grow. Do you have a manuscript or book idea that you would like us to consider for publishing? Please visit advantagefamily.com or call 1.866.775.1696.

To my home team: Krista and Tyler—my all-time favorite players to coach and watch; and Esther—my co-coach and the greatest team mom ever.

CONTENTS

INTRODUCTION 1

CHAPTER ONE 7
Let Goals Be Your Guideposts

CHAPTER TWO 23
Have a Plan

CHAPTER THREE 35
Fill Out a Complementary Coaching Staff

CHAPTER FOUR 49
Fill Out a Complementary Team

CHAPTER FIVE 69
Train Your Team with a Purpose

CHAPTER SIX 87
Let Your Players Play!

CHAPTER SEVEN 105
"Coaching" Your Team's Parents

CHAPTER EIGHT 123
Coaching Your Own Children

CHAPTER NINE 133
Have Fun!

CHAPTER TEN. .149
The Village Chief's Role (That's You!)

ACKNOWLEDGMENTS 167

ABOUT THE AUTHOR 175

MORE FROM COACH STEVE CLELAND. 177

INTRODUCTION

In mid-2016 I was preparing for our 12U All-Star girls' softball season. I was stoked. The team we had spent so much time with, shaping their fundamentals and congealing as a unit, was on the cusp of something special. I couldn't wait to see how much we'd improve and how we'd show other teams that we were now a force in the league. I'd been coaching most of the girls for years, ever since my daughter, Krista, started playing at five years old, and it had been a fun ride. I loved the team we'd built, and I was looking forward to a long summer of softball and spending extra time with Krista, who was blossoming as a softball player.

One evening at home, just before the All-Star selection meeting, Krista casually said, "I don't really know if I want to play All-Stars this year."

It was a punch to the gut. I realized that my intensity with my daughter on the field had been a deterrent to her enjoyment of the game … but I didn't understand the full impact until that moment. I wanted badly for her to play that year, not only because I was excited for the team and wanted her to be part of its accomplishments but also because I valued our time together.

Forget about coaching. I felt like I was failing as a father. I was devastated. Had I permanently screwed up my relationship with Krista? I needed to take a deep breath, think about what I'd learned in my decades as a coach, and once again focus on the village that supported the team's growth and success.

Youth sports has helped shape who I am today. I don't only mean the successes and championships but also the failures, competition, camaraderie, and experience itself. Growing up in a small town in Canada, I was a multisport athlete, but the one I truly excelled at was lacrosse. Playing goalie in the Canadian national championships has been one of my most treasured experiences, the result of a lot of work … and fun.

When my playing days ended, something was missing from my life: that thrill of competition. So I began coaching. I started with lacrosse teams and immediately bonded with the kids. Just as I threw myself into every sport as a player, it wasn't long before I was coaching basketball as well. After becoming a parent and watching my kids, Krista and Tyler, gravitate toward sports, I wanted to be involved. I spent the next decade coaching them in almost everything they played: soccer, baseball, softball, roller hockey—you name it. If they played it, I coached it. For more than three decades now, I've been coaching players anywhere from the age of four to sixteen, from recreational to All-Star to travel teams.

> My real source of pride is that I create an environment where kids, coaches, and parents—the "village" of youth sports—can thrive and have fun.

Youth sports coaches may define success in different ways. For me, the championships my teams have played in are impressive, but my real source of pride is that I create an environment where kids, coaches, and parents—the "village" of youth sports—can thrive and have fun. My goal as a head coach, or "village chief," is to see every kid play without fear of making a mistake, feel like they're part of the team's growth, and consider the season a great experience. Even during a year when one of my teams didn't win a single game, the kids always played hard and had fun. Those parents still refer to them as the greatest winless team of all time. It's counterintuitive to the current win-at-all-costs culture of youth sports today, but it's why I consider every one of my teams a success.

As I worked with kids in various leagues, it didn't take me long to realize—all humility aside—that I was one of the better coaches out there. My teams performed better than most, and the atmosphere I created was more conducive to learning, competing, and finding success. I've also gotten better at my craft over the years because I've refined my process.

Even with my early success coaching lacrosse twenty-five years ago, I had a lot to learn to become the coach I am today. Over the last decade alone, I've coached over fifty teams, run more than 1,200 practices, and participated in more than seven hundred games. Along the way, I've picked up many lessons that would've been handy when I was first starting out.

Much of what I've learned professionally has translated well to the playing field too. Three major considerations have helped me take my career to the next level: owning the relationship, networking, and preparation to fulfill a plan. These translate to coaching youth sports.

Owning the Relationship

Tom Schulte, a mentor and managing partner at one of my first certified public accountant (CPA) firms in Los Angeles, told me, "If you really want to create value, you need to own the client relationship." That helped me understand what I brought to the table not only as a CPA but also eventually as a coach. I learned that my true value lies not in cranking out an audited financial statement or income tax return. My true value lies in solving problems. That's how I became the quarterback for my clients, connecting them with related talent such as estate planning attorneys, bankers, and insurance professionals. This showed me the importance of bringing on complementary talent to help the people I was devoted to.

Networking

Tom also showed me the importance of networking. There's so much we don't know, but we do know others who can help. Meeting new people and taking the opportunity to cultivate relationships, ask questions, and actively listen—this not only grows your knowledge base but also your connections.

Preparation to Fulfill a Plan

Another large impact on my professional and coaching life was Entrepreneurs' Organization (EO), an amazing association that helps entrepreneurs learn and grow. Through its programs, I learned from various speakers and business owners about strategic planning, goal setting, developing a detailed plan, and executing plans effectively and efficiently.

In 2007 I saw this laser beam of energy named Jack Daly speak for the first time. He touched on many themes, but what impacted me most was his presentation on accomplishing goals. He presented an ultimate goal—X number of sales—and asked what you needed to do to get there. He then worked backward from the desired outcome, broke it down per year, then by month, then by week, then by day. How many calls do you need to make? How many successes in those calls? He showed how to parcel out the tasks and build on top of each step while detailing it all within a daily planner.

Jack also advocated for putting each person's role in the context of the greater mission. If each member of a team can see how she adds value or where he fits, it'll give everyone a greater sense of accountability, responsibility, and importance.

> If each member of a team can see how she adds value or where he fits, it'll give everyone a greater sense of accountability, responsibility, and importance.

These three major points— owning the relationship, networking, and preparation to fulfill a plan—have become essential in my coaching philosophy. They're all lessons that come in handy whether leading a project at work or leading a team in practice.

The Village Chief

The more time I've spent in the world of youth sports coaching, the more I believe in the lessons distilled from these three pieces of wisdom and the notion that my own experience would serve many in the youth sports world well. Year after year, I've seen the same types of coaches and the same character traits in parents. Stories I've heard and experienced are similar no matter if they happened in California or South Carolina, Montana or New York, or even Port McNicoll, Ontario.

My goal with this book is to distill what I've learned from more than three decades of coaching youth sports. It can help create an environment where your village of kids, coaches, and parents can thrive in the ultracompetitive world of youth sports. Whether you're a parent taking over a team, a seasoned coach refining your own skill set, a former player transitioning to a teaching role, or anything in between, this book offers a road map for implementing a game plan. Think of it as more than a playbook—it's a tool to become a better team leader. A village chief.

Over the course of the book, coaches will learn to develop a strategy for the season:

- starting the season prepared with goals and a plan (chapters 1 and 2);
- having a coaching staff that you trust in place (chapter 3);
- constructing a complementary roster (chapter 4);
- practicing with a purpose (chapter 5);
- letting the kids play, compete, succeed, and fail (chapter 6);
- handling parents, officials, and your own kids (chapters 7 and 8);
- making sure the kids and coaches are having fun (chapter 9); and
- taking responsibility for it all as the chief (chapter 10).

At the end of each chapter, we'll run down key takeaways for coaching skills and coaching mistakes, and you'll see how these action plans can serve you in your professional life as well.

Now let's turn our attention to before practices even begin, when coaches must figure out the goals that will drive their seasons.

CHAPTER ONE

LET GOALS BE YOUR GUIDEPOSTS

If you don't know where you're going, you'll probably end up someplace else.

—Yogi Berra

In 1993 I took over a travel lacrosse team that was coming off a season that could only be described as awful. The team was underperforming and was regarded as one of the weaker teams in our division. We weren't looking to win a championship. We weren't looking to get into a championship. We were merely looking to compete.

As I was looking at the roster during the preseason, I could see we had some talent. The team's main strength was that they were bigger and stronger than most teams. Though their record didn't reflect it, many of their fundamentals were actually pretty good. At

7

the beginning of the season, I asked the team what they thought we needed to compete. When a few mentioned better defense, I told them they were onto something. We discussed toughness, team discipline, and group effort, and the boys were excited to explore this new identity. We decided to shoot for the moon with a no-way-in-heck-but-maybe-just-maybe goal that year: to be the best defensive team in the province.

To say that was a stretch for a team that lost twenty-five games the previous year would be an understatement. Yet we worked on the fundamentals, and the rest followed suit. We trained for a defensive scheme I was confident would be effective. We discussed the mental aspect of superior defensive teams and rewarded tough defensive play, keeping within our structure and having a team-first mentality.

While we may not have achieved our big bold goal we declared at the onset of the season, we improved significantly by playing sound lacrosse. We were able to hold our heads high because we competed, had fun, and grew as individuals and as a team.

> Goals give you and your team a sense of purpose. They help highlight what you want to achieve and keep the entire village working to get there.

This is the crux of my preseason work: sitting down and establishing goals that will be the key to a successful season. Goals give you and your team a sense of purpose. They help highlight what you want to achieve and keep the entire village working to get there. Whatever those objectives are, I've found that kids are much more grounded and engaged when there are definitive goals. They give a framework for the season that you can check on throughout the year and have a conversation about afterward to discuss what worked and what didn't.

In your preseason work, there are three different kinds of goals you should establish. It's critical that you spend time thinking about what those objectives should be for the following months. These three types of goals are as follows:

- **Coach Cleland's four pillars**, which are a coach's goals for making sure the team is the best it can be;
- **big picture goals**, which are player and team goals for the kids to concentrate on over the course of the season; and
- **the BHAG**, or a big, hairy, audacious goal, something amazing that could happen for the team if everything breaks the right way.

Coach Cleland's Four Pillars

The four pillars are the bedrock of my coaching methods, and they help me draw a blueprint for the kids to grow as individuals and as a team. Whatever their sport, age, or talent level, they're all focused on improving and having fun. These pillars are my underlying goals, and they drive me to train the kids to be the best teammates, players, and competitors they can be, with sound technique and good spirits.

- **Fundamentals.** Cement the real basics of the game in the kids. No matter how old they get, no matter where they're playing, it's all about the fundamentals.

    The exercises have to be age appropriate. Take baseball: when you're starting in Little League, it's teaching the kids how to throw, catch, and hit properly. Don't try to teach first graders how to perfect a major league swing. That's not going to work. Keep it simple. In lacrosse, how do you throw and catch? Where are your hands on the stick? As they get a little older, you can work on more detailed and advanced points, such as underarm and sidearm shots.

Let's face it: no matter if you're talking to a six-year-old or a seventeen-year-old (or even a thirty-five-year-old!) telling them about the fundamentals is boring stuff. But they're also the most critical thing any player can do. Figure out ways to put the "fun" back in fundamentals—make it creative, gamify it, let them learn without realizing they're "working" on fundamentals.

- **Game IQ.** If fundamentals are about training the body, then game IQ is about training the mind. Teaching kids the finer points of the game, to understand positioning, and all the different scenarios they should think about is trickier than basic fundamentals. How you approach these lessons in practices and games takes a bit more planning on your part.

  Players need to figure out their next steps and contingency plans: What do I need to do? Where do I have to go? Where are my feet? What should my teammate (and team) do? That's game IQ, and like the fundamentals, it's developed through focused repetition and practice, being put in scenarios where they have to take the big picture view of the field.

- **Teamwork.** One of the most basic things you can do to ensure the entire group has fun and excels is putting the kids in a team-first mentality. By driving home the idea that each of them is a small piece of a bigger picture, you'll help the kids fully grasp how doing all the right things individually can contribute to the team's success.

- **Having fun.** This isn't even that difficult because the kids want to have fun. It's why most of them play sports. But you have to cultivate a love of the game so they want to return the following season.

No matter how well coaches can teach fundamentals, kids get bored quickly, and the game can seem like a chore. Get creative, and make it fun. Drill something specific, then follow it up with a game—shoot-out competitions in soccer are still teaching penalty kicks. Softball and baseball games where you field a grounder and then try to hit a bucket at home plate trains fielding, arm strength, and accuracy. Or separate it even more—come up with a running game like a relay race. It's secretly helping them with conditioning, and they're having a blast doing it.

These four pillars are my guideposts for navigating through the season, figuring out what to focus on in practices. They help ensure that all my kids will uphold my steadfast rules of giving 100 percent, making it about the team, having fun, and improving. At the end of the day, that growth and success of my kids is the main reason I'm here.

Big Picture Goals

When kids are in the early years of Little League and softball, there's more focus on making sure everybody plays. Generally, when a team of five-year-olds hits, there aren't three outs per side. Every player gets a chance to hit each inning. Since we're dealing with kindergarteners, clean fielding plays don't often happen. Errors are plentiful—not that anyone is keeping track of how many actual outs there are. Let's be honest. It's rare that kids even know who's winning, let alone what the score is! Parents on the other hand ... well, let's save that discussion for later.

When I was once coaching a team full of first- and second-year players, I recognized that as a group, they were naturally good athletes. I instituted something I thought would both challenge and be fun for them: "Hey," I asked them, "why don't we focus on the number of outs we get every game?"

It was like turning on a light. Focusing on those fundamentals with very young kids—throwing, catching, fielding grounders and even line drives—can be difficult and at times scary. But success is infectious. Once we saw some improvement in our outs in the first couple of games, every one of those kids was working to get better for themselves and for the team goal.

Our practice paid off, and it changed the dynamic on the field. My team was soon attacking ground balls like a pack of rabid dogs and then doing everything they could to get the ball to first base. Even more than their fielding success was how they were executing fundamentals, practicing and playing as a team, and having fun. A "perfect" throw from third and then a catch at first from two six-year-olds? It's a small miracle and beautiful to see.

This was an attainable big picture goal that I discovered after thinking about my four pillars. The attention to sound fielding in practices and games unified the team and allowed them to have fun as well as grow on the diamond.

Keeping the four pillars in mind will help over the course of the season in your practices, lessons, games, and conversations with your team. They can also serve you well when you're first thinking about your team's big picture goals. Since you're dealing with kids, you'll likely need a clear idea of where you think your team can go so you can help guide them to their destination.

Remember that these big picture goals shouldn't be something as stark as "winning the championship game." You want teams to be focusing on the process, not the end result. And your players don't need that kind of pressure, especially when small things out of your control could foul that up. Do everything right, get the process and fundamentals down, and the wins and losses will take care of themselves.

When actually formulating and assessing those big picture goals, there are two ingredients that come in handy: understanding your roster makeup and analyzing your key performance indicators or KPIs. Armed with these two tactics, we can create the goals.

UNDERSTANDING YOUR ROSTER MAKEUP

When identifying proper big picture goals for your team and individual players, consider the makeup of your entire roster at the outset of the season, as I did with my six-year-olds above. Think about the following:

- How do you want them to play?
- What do you think they can accomplish?
- What are the critical components of the game your team can focus on and excel at?
- What are the fundamentals of the game, and how are you going to make sure that they improve at them?
- What help do you need to accomplish the goals you will set?

Goals need to be adjusted according to various factors. You'll want to do some customizing before the season begins, and be ready to adjust over the following months. In fact, your goals may morph many times over the season. Along with the roster inspection, consider the following variables when coming up with appropriate goals:

- **Type of team/league.** The kind of league you're coaching will impact the goals you come up with for your players. Here's a brief overview of the possibilities and how they relate to setting goals.

- **Recreational.** Rec leagues emerge from one particular neighborhood or general area and feature teams cobbled together from kids who live in those vicinities. Those teams play each other for a season and likely in a playoff tournament to determine a league champion. These are normally one season long and then done. Many times, a team is given to you without much input, if any at all. You can pick a season goal and add some individual goals based on how long the season runs and the age of your players.

- **All-Star.** All-Star leagues feature the best players from the rec teams, selected after the season. If you coach year to year, there will likely be a core that carries forward. This big picture goal can be a bit more adventurous and longer term. For example, if your team isn't as talented as the competition, you may need more than one season to close that gap.

- **Travel/club teams.** These teams most closely mirror professional leagues: they're privately managed, year-round teams whose players are selected from tryouts or recruitment. They can be a lot more work, generally have a higher degree of intensity, and often come with significant financial investment. There's a lot more year-to-year permanence with these teams, so you can look far in advance and pick a goal that could have long-term aspirations.

- **Age level.** The younger the players, the simpler the goals. A team of six-year-olds may want to focus only on "keeping their shape" (staying on their side of the field instead of the regular beehive formation that typically happens in six-year-old soccer, hockey, or lacrosse) or seeing how many outs they can record in T-ball/softball. Slightly older kids may want to record a shutout at some point during the soccer season or turn a legitimate double play in baseball.
- **Talent level.** Assess the talent level of your team before committing to goals. You don't want to place anything too far out of their reach or way under their skill set.
- **Strengths and weaknesses.** Take a look at the strengths and weaknesses of the players and team. Are they fast? Slow? Big and strong? Are they tall or short, do they work well together, are they better on offense or defense, is it a raw but athletic group? Modify your goals based on your team's attributes.

ANALYZING YOUR KEY PERFORMANCE INDICATORS

As in the business world, you need measurable benchmarks to evaluate whether your team is meeting its goals. These KPIs are quantifiable data points that, put together and analyzed, are a true barometer of success for a project, activity, or product.

In English? Stats help us figure out if we're doing okay. And they're really good for figuring out what your goals should be. It's even easier in sports because there are so many statistics to help you figure out what you should be working on. In basketball, you can look at points in the paint, defensive rebounds, offensive rebounds, or steals; lacrosse options are time of possession, fast break shots, passes, shots in the slot; for soccer, there's quality chances, time of possession, offside calls, number of corners; baseball, well, there's a stat for everything there.

> Stats help us figure out if we're doing okay. And they're really good for figuring out what your goals should be.

But beware: tracking individual stats for kids can be a very slippery slope and in many cases misleading. Ill-informed coaches may use inaccurate KPIs that don't tell the whole story. A girl hitting .700 on her 8U softball team or a boy scoring forty points on his 10U basketball team may not mean anything at all. Context is everything. Their opponents may be of a vastly different skill level. Or the coaches may have their kids working on something specific. Be careful of what stats you track. Focus on what's really important—the team stats. How is the team performing relative to itself and its competition? Is it improving?

No matter the sport, it's going to have similar KPIs to study, regardless of the age level. You just have to figure out how to use them and simplify them for the six-year-olds and make them more complex as the kids get older. Once they're fourteen or fifteen, you can move from focusing on one or two KPIs to using several.

CREATING THE GOALS

So now you've internalized your own goals. You've considered your roster and your skill level. You've taken a look at last year's accomplishments and KPIs (if applicable). What do you think are realistic and achievable goals for your team this year?

After considering them by yourself, get input from your assistant coaches. The assistant coaches are there to complement your skill set, and they may be able to see some aspect of your roster or some KPIs critical to the game that you're not considering. Assistant coaches can prove the most useful by providing fresh eyes.

Discuss team goals with the players, and then ask for their input. Let them brainstorm! Find out things that excite them and keep them interested. If they're younger, offer ideas about what they can accomplish individually and collectively. Unforeseen setbacks over the season are unavoidable, but these conversations will help keep the players and team on track by fulfilling goals even if doing so doesn't result in wins.

BE SMART ABOUT YOUR GOALS

As you conceive the goals, especially as you ask for input from the kids who may stretch them a little, make sure the ones you set down are smart. I don't mean intelligent. I mean **SMART**:

- **S**pecific. Your goals should be very clear and specific. Think about what, why, who, and where as it applies to the goal.
- **M**easurable. Is there a KPI that relates to this goal so you can check in throughout the season?
- **A**ttainable. Pick a goal that the kids can actually achieve. A twelve-year-old stating that his goal is to receive a recruitment letter from a Division I college is an exercise in futility.
- **R**elevant. The goal should fit into the context of the team and league. Ideally, you want your goal to be linked to the team goal(s).
- **T**imely. Put a timeline on the goal. When do you want it to be accomplished by? Once you establish a date, work

backward from there to get a plan of attack.

My 1993–94 lacrosse team from the beginning of this chapter was a case study for the SMART strategy. We wanted to be the best defensive team in the province, a very specific idea. It was also measurable: goals against average, shots inside and outside the slot, and time of possession were KPIs we could track. Was it attainable? Heck, yeah—we had big, strong defenders. It was relevant because we were building a defensive identity for the team, and it was timely because we needed the full season to accomplish it. Our final test would be in the Ontario championships at the end of the summer.

Let's look at some team goals for soccer. Younger teams of six- and seven-year-olds can focus on keeping their shape, staying on their proper side throughout the game, shooting or passing with opposite feet, and switching the field a certain number of times. Slightly older kids of nine or ten can progress to all players scoring or getting an assist. A defensive-minded squad of fourteen-year-olds could concentrate on cutting down their goals against, shutting out a certain number of opponents over the year, and limiting shots on net.

Player goals for soccer would be based on the above considerations as well. Simply keeping up with the pace of the game is a fundamental goal that six-year-olds can commit to, and as they get older, the kids may want to complete passes or cover opponents effectively.

No matter the KPIs or the roster makeup, make sure that the team is excited to accomplish the goals set out. Discuss what pursuing these would mean as a cohesive unit and how each kid's goals will both keep them challenged and fit into the overall team objectives. Once your goals are set, write them down, and share them with the team.

The BHAG

Last, we have the BHAG. It's not a trendy Halloween costume. It's a big, hairy, audacious goal, the greatest accomplishment the team could attain if everything goes well and breaks the right way. You want the BHAG to be a stretch, and the team would have to work their butts off to get there, but if you squint just right, it's attainable.

In 2017 my softball team was coming off a year in which we won several tournaments and played our way into the state championship and Western regional championship games. Needless to say, we were brimming with confidence. We decided that our BHAG would be mistake-free softball (MFS). The team understood that this was almost impossible, but they liked the challenge. It was still critical for the players to know that we would likely make mistakes, but because of our supportive environment, a mistake never led to shame spirals. Rather, it led to a redoubled effort toward no more mistakes. It adjusted the focus to be process oriented and not result oriented.

Once you're able to accomplish a certain amount of success, your growth becomes about self-improvement, measuring your benchmarks against your own levels in the past. When you look at the great teams out there, they end up competing with themselves: their own version of MFS. Can we push ourselves to be better than the previous game? How do we improve every time we play? That's how we came up with our mistake-free softball goal.

Like many goals, the BHAG forces players to focus even more on the precision of their fundamentals. For our MFS, the throw from shortstop had to pop the first baseman squarely in front of her chest. The first baseman would need the proper footwork, to stretch at the right time, and to come off the base ready to throw. That's what we were striving for: perfection.

Of course, you rarely get perfection. Softball is a mistake-filled game. But the BHAG was MFS every single game, so we were laser focused on precision. Positioning, fieldwork, what to do with the ball, what to do without the ball, hitting, baserunning, stealing, and all the rest. Practicing these fundamentals, game IQ, and teamwork over and over kept our eyes on our BHAG and kept us improving and having fun.

GOAL SETTING IN ACTION

Remember that goals don't have to be quantifiable by number of shots made, shots blocked, or fly balls caught. Sometimes, especially when you're discussing the growth and development of kids, those goals are more about the type of player and person they want to be.

I was once working on players' goals with a 14U softball team at the beginning of the season. These would range from a skill like the middle infielders wanting to pivot better around the base or a weaker batter wanting to work on her hitting and/or bunting more. As the meeting wrapped up, one of the kids approached me and said frankly, "I want to build confidence."

This was one of my better players. She'd played for me a couple of seasons before and had gone on the travel ball circuit. It was clear that in the interim, she'd been beaten down by other coaches. It's easy to forget when you're working with talented players that they're still just impressionable kids. It was sad to see her coming to me without the confidence she once had in spades.

"Okay, no problem," I gently replied. "What does that mean to you?" As we made a plan for what her season would look like, we talked about what was important to her—to step onto the field knowing she was going to make plays and keep her head in the game.

I credit her parents with bringing her back to me because they knew she liked me, and she'd performed very well in my system. They figured that I could rebuild her self-esteem by giving her an environment that was competitive but one where she could go for it with no real negative consequences. I was able to build that for her, and we continually had check-ins about it.

At the end of the season, I asked her, "How are you feeling walking onto the field?"

Without skipping a beat, she responded, "Very confident."

I said, "Okay, cool." I didn't have to ask. If you saw her play at the state and national championship tournaments, you could see it. She had command of the field, was clearly one of our leaders, had swagger, and most of all, was having a blast. I would say that goal was achieved.

No matter what the goals are, how audacious or simple, personal or athletic, always make sure that the team is excited to accomplish them. Set the goals, discuss your group and individual involvement, and stay engaged with the objectives throughout the entire season. And that's made significantly easier when you have your plan in place, as we'll see in the next chapter.

KEY COACHING POINTS

- **Spend time up front picturing your goals.** Consider what the team and individuals need to strive for and what you want them to accomplish. It's not about winning; it's about your pillars and the fundamentals. Teach them the game, what to focus on, and how you want them to play as a team and have fun.

COACHING MISTAKES

- **Focusing too much on winning.** Don't get caught up on championships and game results. The real goal of the team should be practicing and perfecting the fundamentals of the game and developing a cohesive team. Being result oriented detracts from what the kids and the parents actually want from sports—to learn and grow as players and people.

TRANSFERABLE CAREER SKILL

- **Communicate with coworkers and seek input from your entire team.** Encouraging others to accomplish their own goals and asking for others' thoughts can help you see things you hadn't before and keep everyone focused on the right things.
- **Set personal and professional goals** for both you and your team. Write them down, and make them SMART.

CHAPTER TWO

HAVE A PLAN

A goal is not always meant to be reached, it
often serves simply as something to aim at.

—Bruce Lee

Benjamin Franklin, the father of time management, is attributed as
saying, "Failing to plan is planning to fail." This notion applies to
many areas of our lives, and coaching team sports is no different.
Having done the preseason work, it's time to create a plan to help the
team reach its targets including the team goals and individual goals.

Let's return to my 1993–94 lacrosse team coming off its tough
season but that had set the goal of being a great defensive team for
the upcoming year. We built on the fundamentals that had begun the
season before, and though we may not have ended up achieving our
BHAG of being the best defensive team in the province, we improved
remarkably. For the 1994–95 season, we wanted to further develop

our defensive mastery but also capitalize on our developing speed and athleticism. We realized we could turn up the gas. Our new goal was to run teams into the ground with a fast pace and relentless pressure. As part of this strategy, we wanted to win every third period of games. It was specific, measurable (using third-period fast breaks, shots, and goals as KPIs), attainable, relevant, and timely.

So the goal was in place ... and now the coaches and I had to design our strategy. We knew we needed superior conditioning. Lacrosse is an incredibly grueling game, and the third period is where the winners win. The more athletically sound team will likely take the game, and we wanted to dominate every third period. What was my plan? All our practices would stealthily incorporate fitness training. It was disguised as games, such as relay races, running with weights, throwing a medicine ball as far as possible, and a grueling drill I simply called the "Richard Simmons Drill." At the end of every practice, those kids were dragging themselves off the floor. But you know what? It worked! When we got to the third period of a game, opponents were in deep, deep trouble.

After you identify what your team goal will be, consider what it would take to achieve it, and then figure out a plan to tackle it. Our answers to those questions were a strong defense; great physical stamina and quick, accurate passing; and intense cardio at every single practice. The plan proved integral to our success.

Without a plan, goals are just wishes. An overall practice plan lays out the strategy on getting to that end result. Concentrating team practices around specific exercises and tactics will help your kids individually and as a group make gains throughout the season. If you're not focused on your process in practices and games, then you're not paying attention to improving your craft. And this goes for the coaches as well as the players.

Individual Player Plans

I've talked about the need for a team plan, but a customized plan for each player is also important. When you come up with the individual plans for the kids, start looking at how those pieces fit into the overall picture. How can each kid contribute to the macro goal of the team? A team that's concentrating on being fit and athletic, how does one individual kid fit into that? A team that's working on passing or shooting, where does a kid who's not so good at those elements find herself? How does a slower kid fit into a fast-paced, high-pressure game? It may take some time and thought to figure out the answers.

> When you come up with the individual plans for the kids, start looking at how those pieces fit into the overall picture. How can each kid contribute to the macro goal of the team?

You may also find timid kids who don't consider themselves good at a certain skill but who may just be cautious because they struggle with self-esteem. Or sometimes, as with one kid whom I nicknamed Bazooka, the issue may be something deeper.

Bazooka was a great kid, but he had a hard time focusing in soccer. He wasn't much of a runner and was no great shakes at passing. From what I saw, many of his previous coaches felt he was a throwaway, somebody to try to hide. But man, when you told that kid to shoot the ball, he would nearly blast it through the net!

I set up a plan to work on his shooting in practice. I consistently drilled him on finding open space, receiving the ball, knocking it forward, and taking the shot. Developing this skill would build him up as a valuable teammate, get him involved, and support the rest of the squad. And wouldn't you know it? He netted three goals in one game at the end of the season and scored in a playoff game as well. Setting up a plan and affording him space to practice shooting gave him the tools to improve and the feeling of worth.

Star players can also work on specific skills, but it helps to make a plan for the intangibles as well, like the girl in chapter 1 who was working on her confidence and leadership skills. At ten years old, my son, Tyler, was one of leaders on his American Youth Soccer Organization (AYSO) 10U soccer team, and during our preseason goals discussion, he said, "I want to assist every kid on this team." This was cool for me as both his father and coach to hear, and we came up with a strategy for that: we agreed that he should focus on his passing skills, his ability to be vocal on the field and direct teammates, his observation of teammates' tendencies, and his awareness of opportunities during games.

Having one of the more advanced kids set up this kind of goal has another positive benefit: it trickles down to the other players. When they see the more experienced kids acting in a positive, supportive way, they internalize that and follow suit.

Having a plan is key for individuals and the team. There are two main ways I keep myself and my teams attentive to our planned goals throughout the season:

- **be prepared** so we can focus during our limited time together, and
- **expect the unexpected** so we can stay flexible and adapt to new circumstances.

Be Prepared

Luck to me is something else: hard work—and realizing what is opportunity and what isn't.

—Lucille Ball

Love him or hate him, Alabama football coach Nick Saban is one of the most successful coaches alive, and many attribute his growing collection of championships to his relentless preparation. He believes that the key to success is precise, methodical preparation on a daily basis and that those who are result oriented will fail. He calls it "the process," and it gets his players to concentrate on the work instead of the outcome.

> The top coaches in any sport are all about preparation. Their success doesn't happen by accident.

But it's not just Nick Saban who believes this. The top coaches in any sport are all about preparation. Their success doesn't happen by accident, and it doesn't happen by luck. If I had a nickel for every time an opposing coach groused about my "luck" with one of my teams, I would have … well, a lot of nickels. Good coaches don't get lucky with rosters or lucky with plays. We make our own luck. Or, as the saying goes, luck is what happens when opportunity meets preparation.

If you put thought into schedules and practice plans for the season, each week, and each day, you'll help your kids build the fundamentals, pursue their goals, and gain an advantage over the other teams. With sound preparation, you can look for opportunity and create your own luck.

One huge pitfall for coaches is not creating specific plans in advance. They walk into practice and announce, "Okay, we're gonna work on bunting today." Or three-point shooting or penalty kicks. They decide that on a whim and figure it could be helpful.

That's no way to run a village. The random, arbitrary approach isn't efficient, and it's certainly not as effective as one that's plotted out. Look at your team's schedule. Over the course of a three- or four-month season, there are a finite number of practices, maybe one or two a week. When you take a long view of the schedule, you realize that—whoa. It's actually not that much time. Do a quick calculation of the hours that you'll get to practice with the kids. It may seem like a lot, but when you compare that to what you want to accomplish, it suddenly appears miniscule.

Figuring out the order of practices becomes very important because there's no way you can focus on every single KPI or fundamental in every practice.

USING YOUR TIME WISELY

Once I realized that the amount of practice per day was just never enough, I began using a few tactics to stretch the day out. Here are a few methods to make the most of the time you have with the kids, streamline practice, and see improvement:

- **Arrival time.** Have the kids show up fifteen to thirty minutes early. This will give everybody time to get settled. You can chat with the kids, make sure they're focused and present, discuss the goals for the day, and initiate a proper warm-up and stretch. All of this before it's your official time to start. Don't waste valuable practice time on the floor, field, or pitch warming up.

- **Postpractice.** Run additional drills or conditioning or cooldown activities to the side. Discuss plays and strategies, and tie them to your goals.

- **Homework between practices.** Encourage kids to watch collegiate or professional games on television. They're a great way for kids to see fundamentals at work. There are a lot of bad habits out there (diving in soccer and basketball and unorthodox batting stances in baseball), but they can keep kids focusing on the details when they watch pros in action.

   Other homework assignments could involve brushing up on fundamentals. In soccer, the kids could concentrate on ballhandling by practicing simple juggling skills, keeping the ball up in the air. Or lacrosse, working on hand–eye coordination and hand control with the stick by throwing the ball at a wall four feet in front and catching it, over and over.

DESIGNING A PRACTICE PLAN

Like formulating goals, drawing the actual practice plan should start in preseason. Based on all the information about your league, players, and goals, figure out what you want to accomplish—which skills you want to develop, what set plays you want the team to master, how your offense will attack, how your defense will prevent—and then work backward. Think about the sequence of skills you want the team to develop. Which skills build on others? Which ones do you need to accomplish certain plays?

We'll get into the precision of practice plans in chapter 5, but remember that this kind of preparation is key to focusing kids and will help manage your finite time. Now when you walk into practice with the kids, you will actually have a plan for the day and can stick to it. Things may happen that will throw you off—one of the drills doesn't proceed how you thought, for example, and you have to modify it on the fly. But for the most part, as you become a better practice planner and coach, you can stick to it and extract the most out of each session.

Expect the Unexpected ... and Plan for It

Everyone has a plan until they get punched in the mouth.

—Mike Tyson

Speaking of calling audibles in the middle of a plan, the wise village chief always learns to prepare for the unexpected. If you think through the scenarios that can impact sports teams—kids missing games, injuries, parents behaving badly, to name a few—you may be able to prepare for them mentally and practically.

I had a roller hockey team of eight- and nine-year-olds that was undefeated throughout the entire season going into the playoffs. As can happen with younger kids, the team ran most of its plays through one superstar, Trevor. Throughout the season, I often tried to prepare them for that dreaded day when Trevor didn't show up. I'd execute plays without him or strategically bench him in portions of games to train the team to function minus the superstar. Sure enough, at the start of the playoffs, we're up against the fourth-seeded team … and Trevor's sick.

The kids didn't freak out. Trevor showed up and wanted to take the rink, but the poor kid just couldn't bring it and sat in two of the three periods. A lot of teams that are reliant on a superstar will fold if that player's out. Yet my kids never quit, and instead of getting blown out with their best player sick on the bench, we lost by a single goal, 5–4.

In all the sports I've coached, I normally set my lineups the night before, but I've also envisioned a kid not showing up the next day. This guarantees I have multiple lineups ready to go. I try to plan for how an injury could hurt my team if we're winning or losing early, how a star not showing up to the game could affect the other kids, or how a star turning up late and wanting to play would impact the others.

Think of some bad-case scenarios that could impact your team, and write them down. Now write down a plan to counteract each. If possible, teach the team the response in practices. When the unexpected does eventually happen (because something always does), you'll know what to do and can calmly go about your business. Your players likewise, because they've trained for it and because they see how well you're handling it, will take the situation in stride.

Of course, there will be things you can't account for. Luckily, because you've trained for adopting a flexible mindset in the face of adversity, you and your players can handle the unknown with ease. If you've made contingency plans, your role will be that of a problem solver in the moment of need. Your players, too, will have a much better chance at staying calm.

Having a plan doesn't happen on its own. Successful teams and successful coaches all have one important thing in common: they create goals and spend time planning. The level of talent and competition doesn't change that fact. They can be fourteen-year-olds on a travel team or eight-year-olds in a rec league, but they should all have objectives and a blueprint to pursue them. A prepared village chief does the work up front, envisions how the players will accomplish what they set out to do, and builds a plan for the season to tackle that. Kids will respond positively and take their cues in both fun and focus from you.

KEY COACHING POINTS

- **Plan ahead.** Think and formulate instead of flying by the seat of your pants. There is a massive difference in mindset and performance between somebody who does the work and somebody who wings it.
- **Start leadership training early.** Developing players often look to the team leaders (normally older kids or some star players) for guidance. Cultivating that and training them to become good models of behavior can benefit the rest of your players.
- **Don't rely on the superstar.** If you have one of the dominant players in the league, train your team to play without her or him. Beyond the threat of accidents and injuries, simply running every single play through the star is lazy. This strategy cheats the other kids and won't work in the long run.

COACHING MISTAKES

- **Creating a flawed practice plan.** Showing up to practice with no plan can be disastrous … but so can showing up with one that's way too ambitious, either for the age level or the amount of time allotted.

- **Not preparing for the unexpected.** Something will go awry; something always does. If you don't think about various contingencies, you will get caught off guard during the season, either by being outcoached in a pivotal game or by not having a full practice plan.

TRANSFERABLE CAREER SKILL

- **Do the up-front work, and the rest will follow.** Establishing a well-conceived project blueprint and planning for contingencies will help you anticipate the unexpected.
- **Develop a detailed plan** of how you'll work to accomplish your goals.

CHAPTER THREE

FILL OUT A COMPLEMENTARY COACHING STAFF

Coming together is a beginning, keeping together is progress, working together is success.

—Edward Everett Hale

When our 14U girls' softball team made it to the state championships, I was struggling with a certain aspect of what's known as the DP/Flex rule, which allows teams to use a designated player and get more kids involved in the game. There are myriad ways to use the rule to your advantage (and disadvantage, it turns out), but for the life of me, I couldn't make heads or tails of a particular situation.

We were hanging out at our hotel in between games, and I

texted a question to my scorekeeper, a woman who was a veritable softball encyclopedia. Within ten minutes, she was in my room with the answer, the pertinent clauses in the rule book itself, and printouts of an umpire's forum where they were discussing their interpretation of the exact aspect of the rule I was confused about.

I walked into the next game with a firm grasp on the rule thanks to my "walking rule book" of a scorekeeper and was able to implement it almost immediately. It had the opposing coaches scratching their heads, but the switch I made got another player involved in the game and helped us secure a W.

> Those on your coaching staff aren't just lackeys you bark orders to. They're part of the village.

Those on your coaching staff aren't just lackeys you bark orders to. They're part of the village. They help form the backbone of the team and are responsible for carrying out your vision of a supportive, fun, and team-first environment. They play a vital role in developing the team and the kids and are an objective eye for every decision you make, from establishing goals to creating plans to constructing the team. When selected well, they bring the skills necessary to making the team well rounded in temperament and knowledge.

A team generally has two to four coaches, often the parents of kids on the team and/or others who enjoy coaching as a hobby. How you fill out your coaching brain trust will change slightly depending on the kind of league you're playing in and how well you know—or want to know—the parents involved.

Coaching Skill Sets

Let's take a look at the different skill sets one might see on a youth sports coaching staff. In the pages ahead, you'll want to evaluate yourself for each of the following skills. Identify your strengths and weaknesses, where you'll want to develop yourself. Later in the chapter, you'll identify where you want your staff to complement you.

- **Technical expert (fundamentals).** This coach knows the fundamentals inside and out: where your hands should be, where your feet are, where you should be looking. The fundamentals are one of my guideposts for the season, and they're the backbone of a player's education and development, no matter the age. If you're not teaching the kids the correct footwork and mechanics, you're doing a disservice to them and the team. It's important that at least one coach has it down pat and can make sure that the staff is teaching the fundamentals correctly and consistently.
- **Game strategist (tactics).** This is the person who's running the game. It's not always the technical expert who's the best at this, though the two roles may overlap. In baseball or softball, it's the person who might be calling pitches, telling the runners when to steal, figuring out when to bunt, who to play and who to sit. The game strategist understands the flow of the game better than anybody else on the coaching staff.
- **Motivator.** Sometimes the head coach isn't the best technician or the one who's got the rule book memorized but rather somebody the kids respond to and gravitate toward. Somebody whose personality is infectious and who makes the players want to work really hard. This is the motivator, and this coach's signature skill is developing relationships.

The motivator's big asset is explaining "This is what we're going to do and why." They believe in the team and each player and cultivate relationships with the kids and inspire them to play hard.

- **Teacher.** Understanding the technical aspects of a sport and teaching it are very different things. Ted Williams possessed some of the highest expertise in hitting a baseball the nation has ever seen and yet was a notoriously bad manager who was frustrated by his players' inability to hit like him. And it's not just teaching—it's teaching these skills to children, not college athletes. You need somebody able to explain the basics like where a kid's feet should be pointed or how to hold her hands in ways the child can understand and replicate.

- **Leader.** This role is often tied in with the motivator, but the motivator doesn't always have the mentality necessary to make the hard choices about removing an assistant coach or having a difficult conversation with a parent. Ideally, you'd see the head coach of the team be both the motivator and the leader, but they may be separate.

- **Communicator.** Communicators are similar to other roles in their ability to explain things, but this is from a macro perspective: making sure the entire village of coaches, players, and parents are on the same page when it comes to the vision and goals of the team, the practice plans and people's demeanor on the field, and what's expected out of everyone.

- **Walking rule book.** I know the rules of the sports I'm coaching pretty darn well. But there are some people, like our DP/Flex expert at the beginning of this chapter, who know every single intricate rule. Or if they don't, they'll know how to research it, analyze it, and capitalize on it immediately.

The older the kids and the more serious the league, the more necessary it becomes to have this coach in your back pocket. Having a walking rule book can give your team and kids another advantage, stop other coaches from cheating your team, and also show your kids the importance of understanding the rules.

- **Jack-of-all-trades.** Whether it's cleaning up equipment, getting the field ready before practice, directing kids, or helping out with drills, this type of person is invaluable and ready to pitch in wherever. This coach is ready to volunteer in any way and happy to do anything to help you and the team.

Upon evaluating my skill sets, I consider myself a motivator, leader, and teacher. Over the years, I've added strategist and technical expert, but it was only through experience, networking, and the wisdom of others that I've gotten there. While you may not be able to check off all the skill set boxes when filling out your staff, some combination of these traits will prove very useful.

When you think about creating your coaching staff, include yourself in that equation. Once you're able to gauge your own value, you can build on your strengths … and shore up your weaknesses by learning more or bringing on coaches who can offset them. Here are three steps in making sure your coaching staff is everything it should be:

- **evaluate your own strengths and weaknesses,**
- **build and develop a complementary coaching staff, and**
- **expand your knowledge.**

Evaluate Your Own Strengths and Weaknesses

So how do you go about adding to, well, you? How do you know who you should bring on to make that top-notch coaching staff?

Start with an assessment of your own skill set. What are your strengths and weaknesses? An honest self-assessment can be tough, but if you want to position yourself and your staff to help your kids and the team, you need to take an objective look at yourself. Can you teach the skills and roles of the sport? Do you have that technical expertise and game IQ? Are you a good communicator? Can you inspire your kids?

Many parents look at the coaching role and think "I can do that" without understanding the skill sets needed for success. Similarly, I've observed former college athletes with excellent game IQ and knowledge of fundamentals but who may not see what they're lacking. Others are thrown into it and have no idea where to begin. No matter your starting point, everybody needs to do a self-assessment. If you suck at something, admit it! After all, only you know the results of the assessment.

When I began coaching basketball, I knew how to teach basic dribbling and passing techniques, as well as shooting and defensive footwork. I had been a point guard and shooting guard when I played in high school, so I was able to bone up quickly. But when it came to moves and strategy for forwards and centers, I was way out of my element. If I had had a bigger ego or been more stubborn, I would have insisted that I could figure it out or wing it. But that wouldn't have been fair to my players, and it would have hurt the team. So I reached out to a former basketball coach and one of the better "big men" in a men's league that I was playing in. They both gave me great info and also helped out at several practices.

Take another look at the list of important roles on a coaching squad. Maybe you recognize certain ones that you fit into, maybe you recognize areas where you'll need to improve, and maybe you can even think of unlisted roles that you'll need to fill to succeed with your team.

Build and Develop a Complementary Coaching Staff

Once you have a strong sense of what skill sets are needed and where your own strengths lie, it's time to figure out how best to overcome your weaknesses. Can you address them by bringing on coaches? What are the traits you're looking to fill out your staff with?

See what talents lie within your coaching pool. If there are coaches you're familiar with who have some of the complementary skill sets you need, then life is much easier. But what if you're new to the league or you've been assigned a team with names you don't recognize? What if your coaching buddies are now your competition?

If you know a coach who's not a parent in your league, go ahead and bring her or him. Many of you won't have that luxury. Most of the time I didn't. Finding your coaching staff will often be influenced by the type of team you've agreed to coach (rec, All-Star, or travel) and how the team is created (assigned, drafted, voted, or selected).

If you're assigned a team, your pool is likely limited to the parents of the kids on your team. Similarly, an All-Star team is limited to the coaches/parents within the league. If you don't know any parents who could fit the roles needed, reach out at the first parent/team meeting. Let them know that you're looking for volunteers to fill certain positions, and detail the skills you think are necessary for success in each role. Think of it as a detailed job description.

If you're coaching a travel or club team, bring the coaching staff, or do some recruiting. If you need to recruit a coach, start with your network. Talk to parents, other coaches, and league officials. In my experience, it doesn't take long to find several good leads. But beware: there may be some parents you don't want to include on your staff. Do your due diligence, and guard yourself against those who don't share your vision.

THE IMPORTANCE OF A SHARED VISION

I once used an assistant coach who had both played and coached at the collegiate level. He was a nice guy, tremendously knowledgeable, and a great technician in breaking down fundamentals. Our coaching experience together started off promisingly: the kids really liked him as a person. But then, a problem: it turns out he had a hard time controlling his temper and would lecture ad nauseam each time the kids didn't follow his instructions perfectly. Each time a kid made a mistake, he'd stop practice to berate the player and deliver a lecture. It wasn't good.

After one practice, I pulled him aside and told him to cool it for the sake of our vision and team environment. He argued with me a bit, telling me he knew what he was doing, that he'd coached college kids. I responded, "Okay, I understand that. But you have to stop the lectures, and you have to stop scolding the kids." I added, "If you can't help yourself, you'll need to step aside and just be a great parent."

Sure enough, it happened a couple more times, and I had to let him go from the staff. However, I also told him that his insights and technical training were great and that I still hoped to use him to improve my own coaching. I also told him that I didn't want it to ruin our relationship. It was a tough conversation—though important for me as the village chief to initiate. In the immediate aftermath, he was hurt. But as our team became much more successful on the field, and as I continued to approach him for his technical expertise, he had some objectivity, and in the end, he realized my decision had been the right thing for the team and his kid.

THE PRESEASON COACHES' MEETING

After your preseason work creating your goals and practice plans, it's crucial to have everyone on the same page. A huge part of making sure that everyone is rowing in the same direction is communication up front. Coaches comes in all different levels of skill, technique, and intensity. That's why it's important for you to be prepared and understand the environment you want to create. Before the season, plan a meeting with the assistant coaches to get their buy-in. Be ready for the conversation so they can clearly understand your vision and how they can contribute. This will allow you to discuss appropriate coach behavior throughout the season and call out violations, as I did with the former college player.

> It's crucial to have everyone on the same page. A huge part of making sure that everyone is rowing in the same direction is communication up front.

Very few people would oppose the vision I'm sharing in these pages—helping your kids have fun, learn and master the basics, and become better people and supportive teammates. But what coaches *academically* know and can agree to versus what they feel during the stressful environment of a game is very different. Pressure can bring out bad behavior in people.

Remember this: it only takes one instance, one coach losing it and railing at a kid in front of the rest of the team, to upend the nurturing, healthy, and fun environment you're trying to cultivate. With a shared vision in place, you can put a stop to that immediately and point to the environment you all agreed to create.

Here are some sample topics to cover in the preseason coaches' meeting:

- **Team identity.** What's going to be your team's style of play? What behavior will you encourage and discourage? What are some strategies your team identity will lend itself to? (For example, a basketball team full of fast ball handlers would fit well with a quick offense that moves up the court and executes a lot of passes.)
- **Environment.** What kind of environment will best support your players in their development? Whatever those important guideposts are for you—letting them make mistakes, encouraging them to have fun, staying focused, being competitive—they have to be consistent for your entire staff.
- **Roles.** Coaches should understand their own and everybody else's role on the staff. They should understand the key skill sets that each of them brings to the table. Address each person's responsibilities during practices, pregame warm-ups, games, and postgame activities. Which lucky coach will address inappropriate parent behavior? Who will address the officials?
- **Treatment of officials.** Not all coaches agree with my

handling of officials. I show them respect and don't often complain or question their judgment. If it's a controversial call, I'll give my opinion on how I saw the play unfold, but they have the final say, and I can respect that. I'm an intense competitor but can be calm in games, so I'm okay when approaching officials to discuss calls. Other coaches may not be able to stay grounded in the heat of intense matches. Those coaches should delegate this task to somebody else.

Expand Your Knowledge

We live in a world of information overload. There are multiple ways to expand your own knowledge and understanding of your specific sport. Here are the ways that have worked for me.

CLINICS

Many leagues require coaches to attend coaching clinics. Some ex-players and overworked parents may view this as a waste of time, but I've always approached it as an opportunity to learn something new. Whether you played the sport at a high level, coached a team fresh off the state championships, or are taking over a squad of six-year-olds still scared of the ball, go to the clinics with an open mind looking for ideas. You'll find some.

Prior to my 2017 season managing the 14U girls' softball team, I attended a clinic run by a guy who was building a great reputation in the Southern California softball circles. Though I was the most senior softball coach in attendance, I arrived ready to learn. Midway through the session, I began hearing a handful of other coaches scoffing at the presentation. The main culprits were former high school and college baseball players who acted like they knew everything and closed themselves off to new viewpoints. They may have thought the clinic was useless, but I walked away with fresh thoughts about technique and three amazing drills that I incorporated into my practice plans.

No matter your experience, there'll be something you'll find that you can use. As with so many areas of our lives, approach these opportunities with an open mind. Don't consider yourself a subject matter expert who can brush off new information. You might learn something.

PARENTS AND OTHER COACHES

I've always been pleasantly surprised by the knowledge and generosity of my players' parents. Remember the village: it's not just the kids who are on your team—it's their families as well. While that can end up being a curse, it's almost always a blessing.

When I first started coaching box lacrosse, I met the kids' parents to determine who might bring value to the team. As it turned out, one of the fathers, Bill, had been the captain of what was considered to be one of the best Junior A box lacrosse teams of all time. He had actually been the coach of the team I had taken over, but he'd stepped down because his relationship with his son, Cullen (the team superstar), had become strained. Bill wanted to respect boundaries and wouldn't have come forward had I not approached him, but he was willing to help.

Good thing, too, because Bill knew some of the intricate skills that I was deficient in. As a former goalie, I needed help with teaching fundamentals that I wasn't familiar with, and Bill became an excellent behind-the-scenes consultant, happy to offer advice and never overstep.

If that wasn't enough, the dad of my goalie was himself a professional lacrosse goalie, and two other parents actively coached their kids in other sports. To say I had stumbled into a gold mine with these parents is no understatement. I was able to utilize every single one of them throughout the season.

It's not just the parents of the kids on your team who can be sources of information. What about the other coaches in the league? Don't be shy in reaching out to find out who's skilled in teaching fundamentals, who knows which online or print resources are particularly insightful. I've also asked to run practices with other coaches regardless of whether their team is our league rival. Sharing ideas and drills is nothing but beneficial for the kids. At the end of the day, it's about turning these boys and girls into better players, teammates, and people. That should be the driving motivation.

ONLINE EDUCATION

Search online, and you'll find plenty of drill ideas, warm-ups, or useful videos. Content providers often upload videos and plans for free or at a low cost. Several have e-newsletters with the hopes that you'll eventually purchase materials or services. When I first started coaching soccer, I came across a website that offered dozens of free drills. I also signed up for their email blast, which included a new drill every week. Over the course of five years, I had piled up an obscene amount of training ideas for my team.

The big question in the Wild West of the internet is, how can you tell which websites are the trustworthy ones? It's hard to discern what's worth your time and what isn't, and it's even harder to decide if you didn't play the sport yourself. The best way to sort through everything is to network. This is the rule of thumb I learned when I became a CPA, and it's a great thing to remember as a coach. Ask around. What are other coaches using? What resources would they recommend, and are they appropriate for the age level you're coaching?

Now that we've discussed how to build and improve your coaching brain trust, we'll turn to how to build the team itself.

KEY COACHING POINTS

- **Be honest with yourself.** Consider your strengths and weaknesses that you can address through other resources or other coaches. The best way to create a stellar coaching squad is by being candid about your skill set.

COACHING MISTAKES

- **Having a closed mind to new information.** No matter how much of an expert you are in a sport, there are always tricks or skills you may be able to develop and use. Don't disregard clinics or friendly advice.

TRANSFERABLE CAREER SKILL

- **Network, network, network.** Some of the most valuable people you'll meet in your industry are your competition. Having conversations about best practices and continuing education can be extremely helpful—and could pay major dividends in the end.

CHAPTER FOUR

FILL OUT A COMPLEMENTARY TEAM

Talent wins games, but teamwork and
intelligence wins championships.

—Michael Jordan

In baseball and softball, when kids are little, the best players tend to play infield. It's rare to see the ball lifted out onto the grass, so the kids who have the hand–eye coordination, aggressiveness, and game smarts are put on the dirt more often to give them opportunities to make plays. Players who aren't as good are more often slotted into the outfield. And everyone, including the kids, knows this.

Everything changes when they're about ten years old and they can hit the ball with more authority. By the time they're twelve, a strong outfield can make or break a team. It's a coach's job to manufacture outfielders out of infielders. That was the task handed to me and my assistant coaches for our All-Star softball team. We had

> By the time they're twelve, a strong outfield can make or break a team. It's a coach's job to manufacture outfielders out of infielders.

talented players who all fancied themselves infielders. If we wanted to compete, we had to figure out who could be a great outfielder and who wouldn't fit in the infield in the long run.

That's when we started to focus on Audrey, a girl I referred to as Sticks. Sticks was a tall girl who didn't have a ton of speed, though she was fairly agile for her height. While she preferred playing first base, we knew it wasn't a fit in the long run, and she became our first candidate for the outfield. We spoke to Audrey and mentioned the move to her parents. They were reluctant since they knew where the "good players" fielded. We persisted, putting the move in the context of improving the team and how important outfielders become as teams get older. Sticks and her parents were cautious but eventually acquiesced.

We began training Audrey on her footwork (e.g., first step back and figuring out paths to fly balls), a crucial skill for outfielders. Audrey was a dedicated student of the game, and if you gave her homework, she'd do it over and over. (She learned to slide with two pillows tied to her legs in the hallway of her home!) By the end of the season, Sticks was our best outfielder. Others, including Kelly, a girl we called Wheels because of her blazing speed, followed. It wasn't long before we had one of the best outfields in the state.

Flash forward to the quarterfinals at the 14U Western nationals tournament in 2017. We were in a tight game against our state rival, La Cañada, up 3–1 in the bottom of the final inning. They had runners at first and second, one out, and their power-hitting catcher at the plate. Earlier in the game, she had hit a home run that barely cleared the fence in center field. When the girls ran in after the inning, we reminded Audrey, "Hey, if you find yourself in that position again, trust your footwork, find the fence, and jump!"

Sure enough, the batter connected hard to center field. Sticks didn't think. She perfectly dropped back, ran, found the fence, jumped, and snow coned the ball. The runners stopped and raced back to their bags. La Cañada was deflated after this amazing catch, and the next kid halfheartedly struck out to end their undefeated season. Audrey saved the game for us in a huge team win. Four years of determination and hard work paid off in that one perfectly executed play. That's manufactured talent at its best.

Building your team with players who can complement one another is just as important as building a complementary coaching staff. Figuring out who can play where, what roles need to be filled, and how everyone can work together is something the village chief has to do.

There are always going to be a couple of stars everyone knows. It's the complementary pieces, and the roles everyone fills, that will make or break your team. Let's take a look at how to surround yourself with a complementary team by:

- **understanding different team formats,**
- **building flexibility, and**
- **making sure everyone has a role.**

Understanding Different Team Formats

Remember that there's different roster makeup for each league type (rec, All-Stars, club/travel, etc.). How the teams are constructed can result in other considerations for the village chief.

Rec leagues typically have regulations that mandate how much playing time kids need to have depending on the type of sport. The number of minutes, innings, quarters, or periods played by all the kids figures heavily into the equation, as do positions and the number of at bats in baseball and softball. Because of these rules, you'll have to create opportunities for your support and development players.

There are generally two ways for regular-season rec teams to be created: assigned or drafted. Each brings different challenges when it comes to filling out complementary talent.

ASSIGNED TEAM

When the kids are young, the most common method of distributing players is simply to assign teams. You'll never be assigned the perfect, balanced team. Instead, it'll be a hodgepodge of kids at various levels of skills, athletic ability, and experience. Your job is to use your creativity to turn this motley crew into a functioning team. There may be ten kids on your soccer roster who want to play forward and nobody wanting to be "stuck" in the goal. You'll need to manufacture talent to make sure all positions are taken care of and that each kid has a role.

I take an unorthodox approach in softball and baseball when it comes to developing players. A lot of coaches often park less skilled kids in a corner outfield spot where they won't see as much action. I try to find kids who aren't strong at throwing or fielding grounders and put them in a position where they may be involved in almost every play—first base. Crazy, you say? Well, if the kid can catch the ball, that's a huge majority of what's required at first. I've always found a developing player who would have trouble anywhere else on the diamond and turned them into a solid first baseman. As long as she can consistently catch, you'll be giving the player an opportunity to contribute and be an integral part of the team, as well as freeing up infield spots for other players.

There are other creative approaches to finding spots for your newly assigned players. Using your powers of observation, thinking outside the box, and selling the fun of other positions will help. And as we'll discuss later in this chapter, finding your kids' superpowers is key.

DRAFTED TEAM

Some leagues prefer to draft teams. But even if you know the kids, you can't waltz into a draft room and wing it. You're drafting talent, but you're also drafting personalities, attitude, and parents as well.

Everyone knows who the top players are. That's not the difficult part. Those kids are only a small percentage of the overall player pool. If you only know which two stars you're intent on selecting, you'll be hard pressed to create a competitive team. How do you bring on

> You're drafting talent, but you're also drafting personalities, attitude, and parents as well.

complementary pieces to round out your roster? Be as prepared as possible through your own research and from other resources.

Eliminate your personal biases and bias from other sources. It's not easy and takes some honesty (and practice), but the better you are at evaluating without prejudging, the better you will be at drafting a well-rounded team. Most coaches will draft with their biases influencing them, so this can give you a big advantage.

- **Use your power of observation every time you coach.** As I often jokingly say, gently remove your head out of your ass, and pay attention to what's going on around you. There are plenty of opportunities to get familiar with the kids. Whether you're doing preseason evaluations, playing games, or watching them, you should be studying all the kids. Having that information in your back pocket will help you in All-Star selection meetings and subsequent drafts.

- **Network.** Your best chance at acquiring new information and learning about other kids is to use your contacts. Any coach with experience with the league's kids can be helpful. I've always valued being able to reach out and ask the right questions: "Hey, I'm drafting this week—tell me a little bit about these four kids." More likely than not, they'll freely give up this info.

- **Beware compiling certain teams.** One of the most difficult teams I've ever drafted and coached—as well as one of the more talented—was the Punching Pandas, a 10U girls' softball team. The night of the draft, I focused on picking the best players available, ignoring complementary skills, attitude, and the kids' parents. I thought my gambit had worked well, yet the other coaches were snickering as we left the draft.

The fact was that my ultratalented squad was loaded with problems. Sometimes it was kids' demeanors and their me-first mentality, and sometimes it was difficult parents, two of whom found their way onto my coaching staff.

As you can guess, the season didn't start very well. Despite my best efforts to get a team with self-centered stars to play together, we weren't even close. I tried to have conversations with some of the players who I felt should step into a leadership position and be more team first. No luck on that front. I stayed positive, and I continued to focus on overall team improvement. Nothing seemed to work. In the tenth game of the season, we were shellacked 14–0 by a team we should have beaten. We ended the first half of the season with two wins, seven losses, and a tie. Parents were upset, and two assistant coaches were openly questioning my approach. I began to question myself as well.

Based on talent alone, we should have cruised to the top of the standings. But what I had done was a classic coach's mistake: focusing on only drafting the best players available.

There are three types of teams you should avoid drafting:

- **All-talent team.** For the Punching Pandas, I focused only on talent and paid for it dearly. As I already mentioned, you're not only drafting the talent, you're also drafting personalities, attitude, and parents. Youth sports are about building a balanced team that works together, fosters camaraderie, and excises that me-first spirit. Putting together a talented bunch of hotshots doesn't mean they'll play well together … and from what I've seen over my years of coaching, it often doesn't. A united, collaborative team will beat the all-talent team almost every time.

- **All-friends team.** I speak from experience on this one as well, though it's a problem endemic to many leagues. It's almost the inverse of the all-talent problem: trying to build a fun team by concentrating on your child's friends. It's a nice thought, but it doesn't work either.

  Practically speaking, if you forego talent and versatility on a roster for the sake of getting all the friends on a team, you end up with a swell group of kids who can't overcome the talent gap. Your "superfriends squad" will likely get pounded week after week and create an imbalance in the league. If you can't compete, eventually your team will get discouraged, no matter how positive you are.

- **Only-kids-you-know team.** I've always looked at new talent in a league as a chance to meet new kids and parents and mine some undiscovered gems. It's paid off every year. Coaches who fear the unfamiliar stay away from new players and new families at their own peril. Do a little work to find out their background, as well as their skill set and attitude. A lot of coaches would rather deal with the devil they know rather than take a risk on the one(s) they don't. That often translates to missed opportunities.

Don't take the safe path all the time. Sometimes the unknown has rich rewards.

THE TEAM YOU WANT TO DRAFT

As you can probably tell, I've gone through some pitfalls that you'll want to avoid. Think about what kind of players you want to draft and what the best strategy is. Every league may be different, but the bottom line is that you want to draft a well-rounded team.

Here are some factors to consider when drafting a team:

- **Key position players.** Even though the team should be solid all over, there are some skilled positions that will make a big difference. They can be a game changer ... or your downfall. If you don't already know, think about which positions in the sport and age level you're coaching are those linchpins. Who sees the most action? The point guard in basketball. The pitcher and catcher in baseball and softball. The goalie and defensive and offensive leaders in lacrosse and hockey.

- **Attitude means a lot.** If two kids are reasonably close in skill, take the one with a positive attitude every time. That trait can prove to be infectious and make up for other shortcomings. Network and talk to the parents. Many times a positive attitude starts at home.

- **Age can be a factor.** If you're in a draft with an age spread of kids (i.e., 10U may be nine- and ten-year-olds), one year of maturity and strength makes a big difference. If two kids are close in skill and attitude, take the older one. The older player will generally develop quicker as a player more often than his younger counterpart.[1]

- **Look for developing players.** When you get near the end of the draft, you'll be looking for your role players and developmental players. Hopefully you've had the opportunity to

---

1   As pointed out in the book *Superfreakonomics*, "Children who are a few months older than their peers at 5 or 6 have more developed cognitive and motor skills, which makes them more advanced athletes," from "The Disadvantages of Summer Babies," Freakonomics Blog, November 2, 2011, accessed March 1, 2019, http://freakonomics.com/2011/11/02/the-disadvantages-of-summer-babies/.

evaluate these kids. If you did, look for positive attitudes, athletic ability, or a glimpse of a kid's superpower. You may find some small hint that leads you to draft one player over another. These picks will very likely have a significant impact on the success of your team, so choose wisely.

- **Don't be afraid to take on a project.** I've heard many times that certain kids aren't coachable. They're labeled disruptive, spoiled brats, or simply problems. Sure, some kids are more challenging, but in many cases, taking a risk on them pays off. (Just don't take on all the challenges like I did with the Punching Pandas!) You may find that with the right approach, they'll become excellent teammates and contribute to your success.

- **Don't forget the coaches.** You'll need help coaching … so consider drafting it. It's not a bad idea to select the kids of the parents you want to coach with.

ALL-STARS

After rec league season wraps up, the coaches convene to figure out the roster for the All-Star team—the best of the best to represent your league against others. This is done by either selecting or voting for the players or a combination of the two.

One of the critical elements of successful All-Star voting is maintaining an honest room. Every coach is responsible for judging the talent with objective eyes. Unfortunately, All-Star selections can bring out the worst in coaches and parents. Some coaches may be pulling for their own players whom they've seen work their butts off to improve, or maybe they're family friends. But are these players worthy of being All-Stars?

Other coaches may act even more selfishly—trying to force their own children onto an All-Star team even if they're undeserving. This is part of something commonly referred to as "Daddy Ball," when a coach gives preferential treatment to their child to the detriment of other players and the team. Daddy Ball coaches give their kids more playing time, put them in key positions more often (even if the talent isn't there), and yes, work their magic to get them onto an All-Star team when they don't deserve it. Honesty in assessment is important here as well. Get rid of any bias, and focus on creating the best possible roster for the pride of the city and the league.

If you're the head coach of an All-Star team, you'll often be handed most of your players based on the collective decision of all the coaches, leaving you with a small number of selections to fill out the roster. This isn't a time to blindly grab the best player available because you're building a complete team. Focus on the role players who'll make the overall team better. If the five best players from your basketball league were centers, you're going to have a problem if you don't pick a point guard.

When I was head coach for the 2016 softball All-Stars, the top ten girls were voted in, and one easy selection left me with a single roster spot to fill. By pure talent, the next girl would have been a catcher who could hit well but was one of the slower runners in the league. Here's the problem: we had two strong catchers on our roster and plenty of hitting firepower. We needed a pinch runner with speed and a high baserunning IQ. That profile describes exactly the player whom we ended up taking.

You can imagine the hurt feelings that came from the catcher and her parents, who knew their daughter was in the running. I made it a point to talk to them and explain the rationale, even if it didn't make a difference. In fact, as I write this, the parents still haven't spoken to me. But it was the right decision, and I wouldn't have changed anything. The player chosen ran the bases all summer, was a positive addition to the team, and helped us win key games.

TALKING TO PARENTS

Keeping parents on the same page, making sure they're looped into the coach's decisions and what's being asked of the kids, is essential. Remember: when you get a player, you get their family as well, for better and worse. Communicating your goals and vision ahead of time gets their buy-in before the season and lays the groundwork for potentially difficult conversations down the road.

> Communicating your goals and vision ahead of time gets their buy-in before the season and lays the groundwork for potentially difficult conversations down the road.

Talking to the parents of the catcher who didn't make the All-Star team was difficult. But it was my responsibility as the village chief to explain this type of decision.

Sometimes talking to parents is necessary to keep the families engaged in the league for the next season and beyond. One year, during the All-Star selection conversation, a coach started putting down a talented player from his team. She was undeniably good, but he harped on her attitude problems and the fact that she wouldn't stop talking. It was enough to sway the room, and she didn't make the team. Rob Graner ("Coach Rob"), one of my All-Star coaches, and I felt the situation might have been unfair.

Coach Rob noted that she could be an integral part of our team's future, and we decided to speak to her mother. "Look," I told her. "I think she should have made the All-Star team. I promise you, if you keep her working hard and progressing, we'll do everything in our power to make sure she's an All-Star."

Sure enough, that girl became one of our superstar catchers for the next couple of years. Was she chatty the entire season? Sure, and she still is today! But was she a good kid who made me (and the team) constantly laugh, and was she a monster on the diamond? Absolutely.

TRAVEL/CLUB TEAMS

Youth sports have become a multibillion-dollar industry, with investors ranging from pro athletes to corporate executives to private equity firms. Corporations such as Dick's Sporting Goods and NBC have acquired companies that specialize in services for youth sports such as online scheduling, social apps, and searchable directories. Youth sports are now contributing heavily to local economies, and new facilities are being bankrolled to attract leagues.[2]

Travel/club teams are a big part of the growth in the industry, and many parents are willing to pay thousands of dollars to have their kids play on one.

There are good reasons for kids to play on a travel team, such as the possibility of better competition and excellent coaching. While that doesn't often end up being true, a parent who does the research can indeed find both of these. If your child is up to the challenge, go for it! Unfortunately, there are also terrible reasons for kids to play on travel/club teams that parents cite: the "fear of falling behind," peer pressure from other parents, or my favorite, the hope of getting your

---

2   Sean Gregory, "How Kids' Sports Became a $15 Billion Industry," Time, August 24, 2017, accessed February 23, 2019, http://time.com/4913687/how-kids-sports-became-15-billion-industry/.

child an athletic scholarship. Talk about goal oriented!

Travel teams and related tournaments have become extremely intense over the years as more money is spent and more pressure is placed on the coaches to win. Parents pay a substantial fee in signing their kids up. That can result in their feeling entitled to voice their opinions and displeasure; it can also lead to constant player turnover. I know kids who have played on five or more different travel teams by the time they were twelve!

The goal for a travel team shouldn't be any different than a rec or All-Star team. There should be a good balance of competitiveness and growth. The focus should be to develop the kid into a better player, teammate, and person and turn those individuals into a highly functioning team. It takes a firmer touch with travel team parents, so being clear about your vision to make sure everyone is on the same page up front and throughout the year is even more important.

The same concepts of how to build a team, the mistakes to avoid and draft strategies, all apply to travel teams as well. If you ignore them, you'll run into problems.

Building Flexibility

Once your team is set, crystallizing the sense of team above individual is key to success. No matter your style or player composition, part of getting them to act as a cohesive unit is building flexibility and depth.

MANUFACTURING COMPLEMENTARY TALENT WITH PLAYERS

You'll almost never have that perfect, well-rounded team, and you certainly won't have one where every player can be plugged into any position at any time. While it's not simple, successful professional teams have a knack for filling in spots when they lose key players. Nick Foles did a pretty good job filling in for Carson Wentz for the Philadelphia Eagles in 2017–18, and some fair-haired kid named Tom Brady launched a pretty decent career with the New England Patriots when they lost Drew Bledsoe in 2001.

This is relevant to all types of teams and age levels. There could be any number of circumstances that require a shortstop to move to second base or a defender to try goalie. In many rec leagues, playing time and position rules force you to play the kids in different positions; as a result, they may end up learning three or more positions during the season. Part of the challenge for the coach is to create the best possible roster that gives kids opportunities to grow and gives the team opportunities to learn and compete. You need to build depth and flexibility into your lineup.

Asking your kids to change positions or cede something to a teammate can also be difficult. It's the coach's responsibility to have that hard discussion, like we did with Sticks and her parents.

It's also the responsibility of the coach to be a salesman for the change. Put the switch in terms of growth for the player and success for the team. Explaining it in this context will more likely lead to buy-in from the players. Also explain the actual specifics of the new position—what it entails and how it's exciting. With Audrey and Kelly and then, several years later, Molly and Breezy, we were able to explain how solid the team would be if we had a "world-class" outfield. Learning the footwork, knowing where to throw, finding the cutoff, and communicating with the other outfielders were major challenges that they were excited about. As they progressed and saw the impact to the team, it drove them even further toward mastering their skills.

BUILDING A STYLE AND IDENTITY WITH WHAT YOU HAVE

If the players have to get used to adapting based on team need, so do the coaches. Connected to building a well-rounded, complementary team is matching your style of play and team identity to what you have. You can't force your strategy on a team that's not built for it. Let's say you come from the Princeton offense school of thought in which a basketball team is run and gun, quick passing and shooting from the start of the game. What happens if your squad is mostly bigger, stronger kids who can grab rebounds but aren't so great at firing passes or constant motion? Don't force a square peg into a round hole. It won't work, and everybody will get frustrated.

Modify your approach based on what you have. Or to paraphrase Donald Rumsfeld, you go to practice with the team you have, not the one you wish you had.

My preferred style of play in goal-scoring sports is to field a speedy group of kids who can run the opponents into the ground and wear them down with relentless pressure. One year, I had a slower, methodical soccer team that was deadly accurate with their passing and shooting. I adapted my style to fit their skill set, and over the course of the year, we worked on controlling the ball, using open space, and moving up the field. We wanted to control the ball greater than 65 percent of the game, frustrate the opponents, and then find opportunities to strike. We solidified strategies for corner kicks and free kicks, knowing that these opportunities would come frequently as the frustration level increased from our opponents. Though not my preferred style, it gave us the best chance to compete. In the end, we had a very successful season, and I learned a lot about a method that I was not used to coaching—and ended up implementing some of those strategies for teams I coached subsequently.

Making Sure Everyone Has a Role

Building a well-rounded team isn't solely about creating a roster of kids to fill out positions. The wise village chief also makes sure everybody feels like an integral part of the system, both kids and parents.

FINDING KIDS' SUPERPOWERS

Another soccer team I coached had a boy who had his pluses … and his minuses. Will focused well and followed game play with ease. He also had a hard, accurate kick, so we placed him on defense because he could clear the ball with a good boot. But his lack of speed was hurting us. One practice, we were down our goalie, and we threw him in the net. And … he was pretty good.

Then we realized that his laser focus had helped us discover his superpower. If we could teach him some of the fundamentals on goalkeeper positioning and taking away angles, he might develop into something special. We taught him the basics, and he ate it all up. We then taught him how to punt better and how to create a quick transition from defense to offense. It all paid off. The kid was fearless and became one of the top goalkeepers in the league. In fact, during our playoff run, he made several saves that most kids his age wouldn't have made. If we didn't have our eyes open looking for kids' superpowers, it never would have happened.

This is a mistake I've seen over and over again: coaches focusing only on the best players and disregarding their supporting players, especially the developing ones.

Many times, these coaches' strategy was to plunk the developing players down at positions where they'll cause the least amount of damage and then disregard them for the rest of the season. Many of these coaches are looking to win championships instead of recognizing the real underlying purpose of youth sports—to develop teammates and human beings on the whole squad, not just a small handful of superstars. In fact, I would argue that it's the bottom end of your talent pool that actually wins championships.

One of my strengths as a coach has been finding a role for each player. When every player has a role, they know that they contribute to the team's success. Once they understand this, they're more likely to embrace their role and excel in it.

It is critical that you develop your entire roster. Pay attention to all your players. The kids who don't immediately show how they can contribute may have a superpower that will reveal itself as long as you pay attention and help them feel like they're an important part of the team. You may be surprised by what you think of when you evaluate without any bias. Take them out of their hidden position, and place them in a role where they can contribute. Then train them so they can perform even better. This will give them confidence walking on and off the field.

Superpowers can come in all forms—bunting, speed, leg strength, hard shots, rebounding. There're plenty of opportunities for these players. You just have to look at them objectively and figure out what they may be good at.

Back to those Punching Pandas, my 10U softball rec team

that had a lot of talent but was getting trounced. With parents and assistant coaches threatening to upend everything, I briefly questioned my ability to get the team to play well together. But with the support of Coach Rob, I stuck to my approach.

I sat the girls down and explained to them how some outsiders felt that our win-loss record meant we were failures. I said that I believed in them and that we could still have a successful season. I then gave them a choice. They could continue to play as individuals and stay at a level well below their capabilities … or they could use the first ten games as a learning experience, challenge themselves, embrace their roles, and give it all we had together.

They chose option two.

The result? We won eight of the next ten games, destroyed the competition in the playoffs, and won the league championship with a resounding 15–7 victory. It was amazing to watch them in the final games as they learned to play as a team and complement each other's talents. That team nearly broke me, but it taught me a lot of lessons and made me a much better coach and chief along the way.

KEY COACHING POINTS

- **Be flexible.** Don't force a team to play to a coaching strategy that doesn't suit them. Adjust based on the team you have.
- **Get everyone on board with your vision.** Kids, parents, and coaches all need to know how the team operates. They all have a role to play.

COACHING MISTAKES

- **Giving up leadership.** If you're not a strong leader who can make tough decisions, you'll be in danger of having other coaches or parents overpower your vision, or you may pick players for teams because you fear the repercussions.

TRANSFERABLE CAREER SKILL

- **Evaluate people without bias.** Interviews are the same as tryouts and drafts. It's amazing what you'll see if you get rid of preconceptions.
- **Make sure everyone feels a part of the team.** You'll create a more cohesive and loyal unit if every team member sees their contribution as integral to the project. Explain how their role fits into the big picture (vision/mission and goals).

CHAPTER FIVE

TRAIN YOUR TEAM WITH A PURPOSE

Practice doesn't make perfect. Perfect
practice makes perfect.

—Vince Lombardi

How do you train your team with a purpose? How do you turn a set number of practices over the course of a season into sessions where you can connect with and get the most out of your kids? What do perfect practices look like, and how can you make sure your kids are absorbing everything you're throwing at them?

Let's look at two very different practices.

In the first one, the players all show up just as practice is scheduled to start. They toss their bags haphazardly over one another and continue chatting as they slowly put on their equipment and cleats or sneakers. The coach stands removed from the players, shooting the breeze with another coach, not really talking to the kids. He finally calls the players together and says, "I don't know, maybe we'll work on fast breaks today?" The kids trudge back to their sports bags and dig around for their water bottles because it'll be a lot of running. This takes a while because nobody knows whose bag is where. Finally the water bottles are out—and now the players have to stretch. The team is now twenty minutes into practice, a drill hasn't even begun, and nobody knows why they're doing fast breaks.

Consider another scenario. At fifteen minutes before the start of practice, dressed teammates show up together, also talking and joking. But when they get to the field, they line up their bags in an orderly fashion, and equipment and water bottles are placed in front for easy access. Still chatting with one another, they begin their warm-up run and stretches, led by a different player each week. The coach moves between the teammates, making easy conversation and checking in with each player. As soon as practice officially begins, the coaches run down which drills they'll be working on that day, how they will make them grow as players and a team, and why. With a clap, the team is up and laser focused on giving the practice their all.

If you saw these two teams on either side of a field, you shouldn't have a hard time deciding which group would get the best opportunity to improve and compete. How you run a practice and how you prepare your players will have a lasting impact on the team.

There are five ingredients a coach can incorporate to get the most out of practices and train their players with a purpose—the purpose of having fun, competing, and growing:

- **setting the tone,**
- **building an interdependent team,**
- **getting the kids to buy in,**

- **creating a precise practice plan, and**
- **honing the mental game.**

Setting the Tone

"You can observe a lot by just watching," Yogi Berra famously said. And kids do a lot of watching … and absorbing. The tone you want to achieve for your team, one that's relaxed yet focused, fun yet competitive, loose yet disciplined, comes from the top down. How you present yourself, how organized you are, and what you demand from the players at that first practice will set the stage for your players over the course of the season.

First impressions mean a lot, and that first practice you have with the kids will leave an indelible mark. As you discuss the season and goals, and what kind of team you're going to be, you're setting the tone and expectations by being organized and demanding that the kids be as well. Kids are impressionable and learn a lot from your behavior. The little things matter, and a structured field or arena or court will be representative of how your kids carry themselves.

Consider the beginning of this chapter, the difference between those two teams. They're both loose and comfortable with each other, but one team came to get down to business, and that intention shows in when they arrive to practice, how they arrive, how they organize themselves, and how they're warmed up and ready to go when practice begins.

ORGANIZED, READY TO GO

Just like making your bed in the morning will set the tone for a disciplined day, the way kids' bags are organized at practice does the same.

Sounds silly? Maybe, but it says a lot about a team if their equipment and water bottles are all neatly set up. It saves precious time during breaks and reminds the kids that they're there to accomplish something. Other teams can have a piled-up mess of bags in the corner but not ours. Softball and baseball bags should be hung up on the fence, bats and helmets lined up, and gloves in front. With soccer, the bags are all lined up on the sidelines, with the water bottles in front. This is part of my emphasis on always looking like a team and acting like a team. If they see how prepared and focused you are and you set the expectations up front, the team's behavior will follow your lead.

Players should be ready to go at the top of practice, not arriving at the court or field not yet dressed or warmed up. It's your responsibility to communicate your expectations and to set that example by showing up early and being prepared and ready to go with a written practice plan.

This attention to detail and respect for the process bleeds into pregame as well. From the first practice, get them used to doing the same stretches and drills to loosen up their bodies and declutter their minds. By the time midseason hits, no matter their age, that routine should be another "breathing exercise." They'll know to do it without even thinking about it. You shouldn't need to be there for them to run through it.

A set pregame warm-up routine accomplishes a few things. First, it warms their bodies so they're physically ready to play. They use the basic skills of the game to bring the sport into their muscles. They practice working together and communicating. It also gets them mentally prepared for the game, centering them through a challenging, physical, repetitive action. An added benefit is the effect it has on opposing teams. Seeing a well-oiled, well-disciplined machine can be intimidating.

The tone is set from the top down. It's not only about the little things such as making sure they're focused and attentive to how they present themselves and their paraphernalia. Whether it's the first, tenth, or twentieth practice, the tone has to be the same. We're here to have fun, but when it's time to focus, we give it our all.

Building an Interdependent Team

If the chief has one lesson to impart, it's that all the different parts of the village rely on each other. Nothing will derail practices and harm your supportive environment quicker than finger-pointing and players who perform in a vacuum. Training with a purpose requires the players to think of the team first and embrace the roles they need to fill. Each of them is an integral part of the team and the environment, and they need to do their jobs for the greater good.

> If the chief has one lesson to impart, it's that all the different parts of the village rely on each other.

Once they catch on that this is a unified front, an interdependent group, and they're playing a role on it—whether they're the goal scorer, the defender, the goalie, the super sub—then things really start to roll. This is part of the expectations and tone to hammer home with the kids, coaches, and parents. We're all going to rely on each other and be the team that acts like a team and plays like a team at all times. Wins and losses, goals for and goals against, runs scored and runs given up—all of that is owned by everyone on the team.

It's easy to point fingers when errors are made. But an interdependent team looks at each mistake as a team problem. I like to put a goal against us into perspective for the team early on. I dissect the last opponent's goal and demonstrate the shared blame across everyone involved with the play. For example, in soccer, before the shot went into the net, who let that midfielder go around them? And who was supposed to cover that player downfield? And why didn't the forwards keep the ball in the offensive zone? Where was the weak side defender? And how did the coaches not strategize against their playmaking? It's a team letdown, so the focus is on moving forward.

Get your players into that mindset that every mistake should be shared by the team. Sure, they'll still feel bad, but they'll recover a lot quicker. And the quicker they recover, the quicker they'll be focused and 100 percent in the game. It works the same for celebrations after great plays—they're shared by the entire team. Most positive plays can be similarly broken down into a team effort.

Getting the Kids to Buy In

Every team needs somebody on staff who can forge relationships with the kids and take the lead on communication. As I mentioned in chapter 3, it's one of the attributes I bring to the table, and it's helped immensely with my coaching.

Why communicate and develop relationships? Why is it so important to have that dialogue between coach and players? Why can't they just jump when you say jump without asking why? Developing relationships with each player establishes a layer of trust between you and the kids, enables them to sign on to your vision, and builds a sense of loyalty to you as their leader and to the team.

COMMUNICATING THE TEAM VISION

Let your players know what kind of team you expect them to be and what your goals are. This holds each player accountable and teaches them a common language of how you as a unit will rise to challenges over the season. You'll support each other and lean into tense game situations. Those moments are a huge reason of why we play, and we should embrace them!

EXPLAINING THE DRILLS

At every practice, before every drill, explain what you're going to do, the precision expected for each rep, and why you're going to do it. Without the why portion, some or all of the kids will miss out on the context of why a drill is important. If possible, and when relevant, tie this into your season goals, your BHAG, and your style of play. When context is added, some of the basic drills that may seem boring will come to life for the kids.

If your style of play is up tempo and high pressure, one area you'll want to excel at is the fast break. To accomplish this, a team will need not only speed but also excellent passing skills; they'll need to be quick and crisp in moving the ball. After all, fast players who can't pass won't get very far. It may be tough for kids to focus on the fundamentals when they're excited to get to the meat of fast breaks. So explain the importance of the skill of stationary, precise passing before advancing to passing with movement and then finally working on the fast break out of your zone. This will show them the critical nature of all parts of the progression. Remind them that precise passing leads to a superior fast break with plenty of odd-man rushes, which leads to more quality shots and scoring opportunities.

It still may not make sense to some of the players until they see

75

it in action, but starting the conversation about it will help.

I often teach a weave in lacrosse, basketball, and hockey, a three-person passing play that drills kids in passing and filling open space. I tried it on a Tuesday practice with one of my hockey teams, the Fire-Breathing Rubber Duckies, and the kids followed it decently enough … but it's complex, and they needed a second (and third) explanation on how to run it. The kids weren't following their passes or were bumping into one another, not quite sure how the play would work. By their next practice two days later, they were able to run it somewhat functionally, though it was still clumsy. Sure enough, that Saturday, during our game, three kids came out of our zone, performed a perfect weave, and scored. As they were celebrating after the goal, one of the kids who I had been unsure would ever nail it, looked at me and asked, "Was that the weave, Coach?" I high-fived him and said that hell yes, it was.

Clarity on how you want your players to run a drill and the (age-appropriate) precision needed is important. Show them the expectation for every step of the drill. Don't take it for granted. It may seem simple to you, but the kids you're dealing with are still developing their fundamentals and game IQ. Oftentimes, when kids mess up drills, it's not necessarily their fault. Coaches should stop the drill, take the blame for not explaining it well, and ask to try it again; and then step by step, show them how to perform it. While the drill may prove to be too complex, it could also simply take a little time to sink in, but when it does, as with the weave, the results may be electric.

BUILDING A RELATIONSHIP

We often forget this when we watch professional athletes play, but those women and men playing sports—they're just like us. They're people who experience happiness, sadness, regret, desire, panic, everything. Coaches must never forget that about their players. So take the time to know each of the kids on your team.

This may mean you're not running ten drills over the course of your practice, but that's okay. A lot of practice is about building relationships between teammates and between coaches and players. Make a point of connecting with them. There's downtime in practice where you get a little more time to hang with the kids. Between drills, or even during drills, pull one of your kids aside and connect with them. Get to know them, and ask them about their motivations, about what they want to accomplish, or maybe just about their favorite video game.

This is the integrated approach toward team practices: talking with the kids and building the team together instead of a keeping a command-and-control relationship. Having them know what the team's philosophy is, explaining why you're executing the drills you are, and forging a real connection with them builds loyalty to the team, coach, and each other. It's that connection that will have the kids playing their hearts out for you and the team. And this is particularly important because each and every kid is an extension of your interdependent team.

Creating a Precise Practice Plan

It seems like everybody is aware of the ten-thousand-hour rule popularized by Malcolm Gladwell's book *Outliers*. Many of these people believe that if you get your kid up to ten thousand hours of practice, they are destined for greatness. But it's not that simple. It's not just logging hours in mindless reps, like casually shooting free throws or taking halfhearted swings in batting practice.

It's critical that those reps are focused and precise. Train your players in their fundamentals very precisely and in exactly what they need to improve. Whether your players are practicing free throws or taking batting practice or setting up for corner kicks, make sure they're actually committing to the exercise and understand the age-appropriate precision that is expected. Practicing over and over again with precision will get them to the point where the motions become as simple as breathing. So when it's game time, these moments are second nature to them—they can rely on their training and act out of instinct.

> It may be practice, but it's also an opportunity to replicate gamelike conditions.

It may be practice, but it's also an opportunity to replicate gamelike conditions. Free throws never come at a moment of rest and relaxation. They almost always are taken under pressure, after you've run up and down the court forty times. That's why I like to pepper in free throws throughout my basketball practices. After a player has just busted his ass running down the court, he has to take a couple of free throws while teammates stand around the key making noise.

Just as I learned from that inspiring speech from Jack Daly mentioned in the introduction, if you've got something to accomplish, work backward. You should already know what fundamentals you want to work on and the sequence you have planned. Now, how are you going to get there with the allotment of time you have? Break it down by chunks, monthly, then weekly, and then form an actual practice plan for each day.

Each weekly practice plan should leave room to discuss the prior game. Debrief. With a few days of hindsight, players are able to be more objective and can consider what went right, what went wrong, and what they can learn going forward. It's likely that something happened in the previous game that could make its way into practice today, especially if it exposed a team weakness or a strength you want to build on.

If your opponents in this past weekend's basketball game employed a full-court press and you hadn't planned a counterstrategy to that yet, spend some time in the next practice working on breaking presses. Same thing in softball: if you just lost to a team that small balled (through slap hits and bunting) your team to death, then practice defending against it.

And I can't stress this enough: write down your daily practice plans. This is crucial. If you've written down what you want to accomplish in each practice and you're able to communicate it to the team, you'll have a much better chance of bringing the plan to fruition. Don't wing it, and don't rely on your memory. A good practice is the product of a clear, efficient plan, and that piece of paper is your script for the day.

There are five key points to highlight when creating a practice plan.

- **Practices need to be precise and focused.** You need to focus on exactly what you want to accomplish each day, each drill, and for each player, and it's up to you to make that happen. You and your coaches need to communicate to your players what the goals of each day will be and what each drill will accomplish.
- **The level of practice should be at the level of the more skilled players on the team.** I've seen coaches run

sessions at the level of the average player or even below that. I believe that's a mistake. I always practice at a higher level. Contrary to the idea that this will intimidate the ones having difficulty, I've found that each player strives to jump up to the level above.

There will be, however, developing players for whom any level of practice can be intimidating. They struggle with many of the drills because they're still learning the fundamentals. For those, I've invented something called Early Club, which leads me to the next point.

- **The bottom half of your team wins championships.** Stars can often cancel each other out in competition, which is why it's so important for your role players to bring it. Early Club came from my realization that those kids on the lower end need some individual attention, attention that I can't offer them in a group practice. Now, only coaches who want to invest this kind of extra time can run Early Club, but it pays off because the bottom half really does win championships.

  Early Club is a prepractice session, starting about thirty to forty-five minutes before team practice, where I invite (through the parents) the kids who are having trouble picking up the basics. Usually it's about two to four players, and they're able to get the attention they need to work on core skills at a slower pace, so they can get precise reps in before regular practice begins. Early Club helps build their fundamentals and also gives them a bit of a head start on the practice to come. This one-on-one time I'm able to devote to them pays off in building skills as well as loyalty. The parents are thrilled because

I'm taking extra time to help their kids improve and contribute to the team's success.

Early Club doesn't have to happen before a practice. It could happen after a game, on a weekend, whenever. But the important thing is to take the extra time to build a kid's confidence. Often you'll see assistant coaches and some of the star players show up and help as well.

- **Disguise your conditioning.** A trick to getting kids in better shape is for them *not to know they're getting in better shape*. Disguise it. Gamify it. Take cardio in baseball or softball. Have the kids run the bases, taking the turn at first to stretch a hit into a double. Show them where their footprints are and how wide a turn runners should have. Continue to talk about their paths through the bases as they leg out singles, doubles, and triples. Soon enough, they've been running all practice and are not even aware they've done it.

  For soccer conditioning, consider relay races—either short ones where they rip through cones or long, sprinting ones where they kick a ball over the course of the field. It's amazing how much harder kids will work when there's a competition on the line. Each side is cheering their hearts out, and when they finish the race panting and sweating, they don't even realize how much exercise they've just had.

- **Remember that the practice plan is a living document.** As a coach, you're constantly evaluating and adapting to fit the needs of your team and the individual players. Just as you want to talk about the prior game and work on weaknesses exposed by another team, you also want to

> have some flexibility to take in how the kids are feeling
> and how to expect the unexpected.

Honing the Mental Game

Ninety percent of the game is half mental.

—Yogi Berra

One of my all-time favorite kids to coach was Coach Rob's kid, Erin, whom I referred to as Graber. I'd been coaching her since the Green Grasshoppers soccer team, when she was five, and even in those early years, Graber was a special player. She was always a gamer: competitive, athletically gifted, highly coachable, and a great sport.

Softball was no different. She had a very high game IQ; was our star shortstop, our leadoff hitter, a great teammate, and one of our leaders; and pitched in some of our most important games. Our 14U All-Star softball team sported an ace, Marlee, who had a couple of inches and maybe fifteen pounds on Graber. Marlee was able to intimidate our opponents with her size and overpower batters with the pure speed and movement on her pitches. Graber didn't have that. What she did have was pinpoint control and off-speed pitches, including a devastating changeup. However, she could get a little jittery ahead of games.

Our Western nationals championship semifinal game was a rematch against one of our toughest opponents of the season: a fantastic travel ball team from Washington State. Before the game, Graber was feeling the stress and pressure of the moment. I asked her to take a little time during warm-ups to simply sit and picture her pitches. She rolled her eyes, but I kept on. "Okay, I want you to envision your fastball, and I want you to pick a corner." We continued like this for five or ten minutes, me simply coaxing her out of her head and her simply thinking about pitch location and how different scenarios would feel.

Before long, her jitters were gone. It was a simple centering exercise that calmed down her nerves and let her visualize success. She just needed to get her mind off the stressful moment, take a breath, and refocus on the challenge ahead. I finished our conversation by reminding her, "We have the best defense in the state. If they hit the ball, we'll make the plays."

Game time rolls around. Graber gets to the mound and proceeds to pitch six shutout innings on our way to an 11–2 victory. I could rattle off another dozen or more games where we handed Graber the ball and looked to her to lead us into a huge game. Once her nerves were settled, she never disappointed.

It's becoming more and more common in professional sports for franchises to nourish the mental and psychological side of athletes. Just about every National Football League or Major League Baseball team has a psychologist on staff, and visualization and other mindful approaches such as yoga and meditation are becoming as commonplace with pro athletes as physical training or nutrition.

Doesn't it make sense that such approaches to the mental aspect of the game should be taken up with kids as well?

Remind the girl on the mound that her team has her back. Remind the boy playing forward where to be on a fast break, or the girl playing center where to send a jump ball, or any number of your players where their minds should be at any given moment. It'll heighten their game IQ and also help center them and keep them breathing at moments of high pressure.

With enough reinforcement and repetition, each of them will

know exactly what to think … or at least how to think in a positive, focused way.

VISUALIZING AND PREPARING FOR SUCCESS

Giving girls and boys the mental as well as physical tools to handle the tension of a sport is crucial. Talk with them, and explain how heightened game drama is why we play: for the adrenaline rush and the fun that comes with that. Part of creating the supportive environment is inspiring the team to lean into those high-pressure situations.

From day one, I talk about that with my players. It's a constant discussion of what it'll be like in the middle of a game, when the pressure is on—batting with the team down a run and two runners on base or taking a penalty kick with the game tied—and what it's like to want that challenge, no matter the result. Teach them to slow the game down, embrace the challenge, and think about how they can be the difference maker. Win or lose, we'll have the opportunity to take part in thrilling moments.

Taking a moment to breathe and visualize these in-game scenarios not only helps the kids picture their success, it also lets them calm down and center themselves.

To mentally prepare them for game time, walk them through different scenarios. Where should they be on each play? What should they be thinking during these moments? Like the physical fundamentals, the more you work on the mental aspects, the more they'll become second nature to the players.

Your goal should be to reduce the intensity in those big game situations instead of adding to it. There are a lot of coaches who take it up a notch when weekend game time rolls around. They might be even keeled and relaxed under nonpressure circumstances; maybe they ran practices like that, a bit loosey-goosey. And then bam—it's competition time, and the brakes are off. Their tension ratchets up, and all of a sudden the players are tight and anxious about failing.

In my experience, it is better to ease up. The pressure of the game is always enough for the kids. Increasing the intensity level often backfires, and all the fundamentals and training you've done could go out the window. Don't ask for extra effort during the game. Demand it all

> Don't ask for extra effort during the game. Demand it all season long in the practices.

season long in the practices. Hold the kids accountable throughout the season. They'll be better prepared mentally when games arrive. Trust the work you've done through your practicing with precision and purpose, stay in that familiar zone of effort you've built throughout the year, and they'll rise to the challenge.

KEY COACHING POINTS

- **Have an organized, flexible practice plan,** and make sure it's in writing. With only a certain number of practices per season, you need to cover all the key fundamentals multiple times.
- **Demonstrate and reinforce the level of precision** that is expected in each drill and rep.
- **Communicate your process to the kids.** It will build loyalty and trust and give them ownership over their roles.

COACHING MISTAKES

- **Winging it.** Even if you're a seasoned coach or former athlete in the sport, don't assume that you can walk onto a field and brainstorm good drills on the spur of the moment. You can't improvise your way to success.

TRANSFERABLE CAREER SKILL

- **Being prepared to run a meeting serves you well.** It shows a sense of discipline and organization that will have coworkers emulating and trusting you. People learn from the top down.

CHAPTER SIX

LET YOUR PLAYERS PLAY!

Play gives children a chance to
practice what they are learning.

—Fred Rogers

I was coaching the Puffy Annihilators, a U10 girls' soccer team, and we were approaching the end of a successful season. Even though our record was just a touch above .500, I considered our season an overall success because we had created a supportive environment where players bolstered each other and weren't scared of making mistakes. It was great to see the girls helping each other through their ups and downs, and heading into the playoffs, we were playing the best soccer of our season. We won our first two playoff games and were now up against the top team in the league in the semifinals.

This team had the best player in the league (by far) and was rarely challenged throughout the year. They also had a coach who expected perfection and was incredibly vocal when he thought that wasn't happening. This coach had set up a one-dimensional playbook: defend and then get the ball to the best player in the division. Like Mariano Rivera's cut fastball, you knew it was coming, but you still couldn't defend against it. No team in the league had been able to stop them. In fact, they had destroyed us 8–1 earlier in the season.

By the playoffs, however, we were a very different and much-improved squad. Each girl had embraced her role(s) for the team. And for this particular game, we had two kids who I thought could make a huge impact. First, there was our goalkeeper, Krista, who had quietly developed into one of the best keepers in the league. Few teams noticed this because she went about her business cutting angles down and knocking balls out of the net without any fanfare. Instead of sitting back and trying to make a highlight-reel save, she would challenge shooters and coolly make the stop.

My other secret weapon, Kaeley, wasn't one of the top players in the league. She wasn't even one of the best on our team. While she may not have been a perfectly refined player, she was athletic and fast and had no problem getting physical. Kaeley had played both soccer and softball for teams that I had coached, so I knew she was perfectly suited for her assignment: to play the role of a pest to the opponent's superstar.

Our team was built on solid defense, methodically bringing the ball out of our zone and then creating opportunities for several of our kids to make shots on goal. But this game was a little different. Kaeley was to be a constant thorn for that superstar, never leaving her side. If Kaeley got beat, the other players were instructed to jump in and slow the superstar down long enough for Kaeley to get back into position and sideline their only real offensive weapon. If they were going to beat us, their star was not going to be a part of it.

We scored first, and I immediately saw the telltale cracks in our opponents' demeanor. We scored again, making it 2–0, and their frustration began to mount. Their superstar got the ball, sliced through four of my players, and laced a shot into the top corner of our net: 2–1. My team was unfazed, supportive of each other, and dedicated to our game plan. But they knew their hands would be full all night.

When we scored our next goal, the opposing coach upped his intensity, barking louder and louder at his kids. They redoubled their efforts to get the superstar the ball, but great help-out defense and two big saves by Krista kept our lead. Frustration began to boil over for the coach. He was now pointing out all their mistakes and scolding them for not executing their strategy. The superstar was also getting frustrated not only from being tied up all game and her coach losing his mind but also from her dad yelling at her from the stands. The score was only 3–1, but we may as well have been up by 50. Everything started going our way. We gained confidence, and our opponents were afraid of what their coach was going to yell next. As a result, you could see that they were playing tentative and scared. We got up to 5–1, and with one final, frustrated push, the top player ended the game with a perfect shot from 40 feet out. Too little, too late. Final score, 5–2.

What happened to that team is a pattern that's happening in youth sports across North America. Sports can be a great, entertaining outlet for kids to enjoy themselves, play hard, have fun, and grow. I feel that outlet has become more serious and tense now— and not just for that coach who had no problem yelling at his kids who were up against a strong defense. It's serious for parents, too, who seem to be in an arms race against other parents to get their kids into a special club and then increase the pressure over and over again.

For all the thousands of dollars parents spend on getting their children onto travel/club teams in hopes of scholarships, it may make more sense to set up a college savings plan in the child's name, and then let the kid play a sport for fun and individual growth.

What some coaches and parents seem to forget is why kids want to play in the first place. Every time they throw a fit when the kids make a mistake, they're creating an obstacle to the player's development.

Early on in my coaching career, I fell into the habit of trying to be a puppet master for my players. Soccer, basketball, lacrosse, I'd be on the sidelines telling them what to do; how they should move the ball to the left, now to the right; when to pass; when to shoot; and on and on. And then one day I realized that some of the kids weren't listening, some completely relied on me (and froze if I didn't tell them what to do), and most of the others were struggling to understand what I was saying.

And then something clicked. What if I gave them a break? What if I just shut up and let them play the game? Get out of their way, and encourage them to make decisions, make mistakes, and learn from those mistakes. When you do this, watch the team because something very cool happens: leadership and game IQ develop. Try it for one period, one quarter, or one half.

> That should be the directive for every coach.
> Shut up, and let your players play.

That should be the directive for every coach. Shut up, and let your players play. Set up the environment for your kids to succeed, get everybody on board, and then protect that environment with all your might.

So how do you get your players to play?

- **Create an environment where your players aren't afraid to fail.**
- **Get support from the coaches (and parents!).**
- **Set the example.**
- **Pick your moments.**
- **Recognize that some days just ain't your days!**

Create an Environment Where Your Players Aren't Afraid to Fail

Recognize it, admit it, learn from it, forget it.

—Dean Smith, on what to do with mistakes

Think about what you've done as a coach: you've built up the roster, you've had a look at what the players' strengths and weaknesses are, and you've thought about what kind of team they're going to be. You've constructed the coaching staff, complementing your own attributes and making sure all the necessary skill sets are accounted for. You've created goals for the players individually and as a team. You've established a precise practice plan, equipping your players with physical skills and mental tools. With all this work you've poured into forming the right process, now it's time to take a step back and let them learn by doing. Come game day, it's time to get out of their way and watch them perform. Trust that they've practiced with precision, and then support them as they come together as a team and play.

Creating the environment where your players are not afraid to fail starts at the first practice and the first team meeting. As I outlined in chapter 1, the four rules for the teams that I coach are that they give 100 percent (the go-for-it mentality), act team first, have fun, and improve. These four guidelines help create that supportive environment that—guess what?—encourages them to make mistakes, fail, and learn.

It's important that they hear that from their coach consistently throughout the season! The opportunity to fail without negative consequences is one of the most critical elements of playing in your village. I would go so far as to say it's important in every area of a kid's life. Give them that ability to play the game and make mistakes, and when they do, support them. Encourage them to go out and test themselves again. Help the team learn from those mistakes, continue to try, and keep having fun.

Let the idea sink in for a moment. A safe, supportive environment that allows kids to make mistakes and not get yelled at; the freedom for a player to try something that he or she just might excel at. Once the kids see that there's no risk of shame or punishment, they might gather enough courage to dive for a grounder in the hole. Or try a bicycle kick in soccer. Or try dribbling a basketball with the opposite hand when they hadn't had the confidence before. It will likely start with your superstars, and their bravery will give the next bunch of players the encouragement to go for it. Pretty soon, your entire team will be stepping up and making a play that they may have once thought was impossible.

Maybe it works. Or maybe it fails—and when the coach doesn't lose his mind and actually applauds them for trying? Then the players see they have the freedom to keep on trying.

It can be difficult to get kids to accept the concept, as most of them have faced harsh consequences for mistakes before. It won't happen overnight. Be patient and consistent in discussing the go-for-it mentality and positively reinforcing the effort to make it happen. It may take several weeks, but it will be worth it when you get there!

FEARLESS CULTURE

The environment where players are not afraid to fail is a powerful element for growth. Ed Catmull, the cofounder and president of Pixar, made it one of the central messages in his book Creativity, Inc. "If you create a fearless culture," Catmull wrote, "people will be much less hesitant to explore new areas, identifying uncharted pathways, and then charging down them."[3] In a fearless culture, your team can be focused on making plays—picking a kid off at third base, executing a weave, or converting a corner kick—rather than on avoiding mistakes.

You know those teams where fear is in the air. I guarantee that after the Puffy Annihilators' opposing coach went to town on his players, our opponents were more concerned about screwing up than following the game plan.

Do coaches and parents think the kids thrive under such circumstances? When everybody is calm and cool, most people would say no. But if you watch a youth game this weekend, many of the coaches and parents certainly don't appear to think so.

Just take it from Catmull, who also wrote that "in a fear-based, failure-averse culture, people will consciously or unconsciously avoid risk. They will seek instead to repeat something safe that's been good enough in the past."[4] For our soccer opponents, doing the safe thing sure wasn't good enough this time.

Fear-based culture can hamper even the most talented teams.

---

3   Ed Catmull, *Creativity, Inc.* (New York: Random House, 2014), 111.

4   Catmull, *Creativity*, 111.

Our 14U All-Star girls' softball team was in a close game with a rival that had beaten us every year—often by double digits. Since the kids were seven years old, this team had been stacked with talent and always one of the favorites to win our district and then compete for the state championship. However, their management style was the polar opposite of ours. Over the years, that team had several different coaches, but the program was the same: yell, intimidate, and punish the kids who make mistakes. This season was no different for them. They were loaded with talent and still employed an aggressive coaching style. For us, however, there was a very different feeling in the air. Though we were down early, we had a pair of base runners on and were threatening to take the lead when the opposing manager yelled out of the dugout to his third baseman, telling her to "wipe the smile off her face" and that "it was time to go to work."

It was like the jukebox record skipped. The entire diamond felt the pressure increase on the opposing team, and when our next batter put the ball in play for a base hit, I knew it was our time to strike. We not only took the lead that inning, we put the game away with several hits in a row. That perennial powerhouse of a team never came close to beating us again. And each time we played them, the opposing coaches tried to "inspire" their players by getting more intense, and each time we came out victorious. In fact, we outscored that team a combined 36–3 after the wipe-that-smile-off-your-face game.

LOOSE CANNONS

Sometimes you'll get those kids whom you give an inch and they'll take a mile. The second baseman who dives for a ball that's hit toward the shortstop or the guard who's chucking up three pointers from half court. Or a lacrosse attacker who tries to execute a between-the-legs shot.

There's being aggressive, and then there's hotdogging. One is productive, and one is counterproductive. Shaming the kids isn't the right way to reach them, though. Pull them aside, tell them you love that they're having fun and going for it. We don't want to squash that kernel of fun. Goodness knows there are so many areas of their lives where they don't have the freedom to push the envelope. At the same time, tell them that the whole team has to be on the right path toward learning something and that clowning around like that can be a distraction. Reframe their thoughts by reminding them of the team BHAG, team goals, or the role they play in the team's success.

Get Support from the Coaches (and Parents!)

If I acted in the classroom the way most coaches do with their players in youth sports, I would be fired immediately.

—Steve Hopkins, Torrance All-Star coach and schoolteacher

It's all well and good for coaches to be theoretically on board with an environment where players are not afraid to make mistakes. In practice, however, especially in the heat of the moment, it may be a different story.

I find it important to get buy-in from the coaches at that initial meeting with them, making sure they're on board with our team philosophy. It is critical to agree that everybody will be able to support the kids when they try something and fail. Much like the conversation with the kids, I look at the coaches and ask them to repeat back to me, "We're going to go for it, and we're going to make mistakes, and that's okay."

The same principle applies to parents. At the first parent meeting, set the tone, and get agreement from each parent. Look each of them in the eyes and have them state, "Yes, I will smile and support my child when they make a mistake." It's not like signing a piece of paper and not believing it. You'll be able to tell if Jaxon's dad is only giving you lip service while actually rolling his eyes.

Actively getting this buy-in sets the foundation for holding coaches and parents accountable. They're aware of the importance of the environment you're creating and their role in it. It also lays the groundwork for your calling out their bad behavior down the road.

In the calm before the season, every parent agrees that making mistakes is a critical part of learning. It's easy for them to say that they understand the supportive atmosphere you're creating, but when it's game time and their kid misses a shot or a call goes against our team that they think was bull, some parents won't be able to help themselves. You'll quickly find out which parents struggle to keep their commitment, often during the first game. Others take a couple of games to come out of hiding!

Negativity has a snowball effect, and even one instance of it can do significant damage. Coaches have to believe in their positivity as well. I can't tell you how many times I've seen a kid make a mistake and witnessed a coach throw a clipboard or make some huge gesture or face on the sidelines but then clap the player on. Or bring the player over in the dugout and rip them a new one and then end the tirade with "Okay, good job. Let's go get 'em." You can't just put the words of positivity around the environment and not truly believe them. The kids will understand you through your actions.

It is never okay to berate, belittle, or mock your players. Full stop. That kind of behavior is frowned on in most areas of life but for some reason is given a pass in sports, from youth on up to professional. Why is it okay for an adult to act this way toward a child when it's linked to a sporting event?

> It is never okay to berate, belittle, or mock your players. Full stop.

I had a discussion a few years ago with a coach I'd been in leagues with over the years. He was proud of his old-school label, which translated to "his team, his rules" and throwing fits whenever his players didn't execute properly. He told me he was frustrated with a team he was coaching. He knew that the talent was there but couldn't understand why they weren't performing to their capabilities. He asked for my feedback.

It wasn't an easy conversation.

I told him that I didn't think his yelling at and punishing the players was getting them to play well. He, in turn, groused about how soft kids are these days, how they need to know who the boss is. I countered that you can still hold players accountable without making threats. He flatly disagreed and said there needed to be tough consequences.

And on and on.

It was like talking to a brick wall. We never coached together again. Despite his deep knowledge of the sport, his teams constantly underperformed, and there always seemed to be a reason other than his approach with his players.

You can hold players accountable without acting like a jerk. Take them aside, and talk to them with respect. Ask how the game or certain plays could have gone better. In postgame huddles or practices, take bad execution as an opportunity to have a dialogue, and help the players learn rather than using that time to yell at and scold them.

Set the Example

I'll say it again: kids take their cues on how to behave from the top down. And that includes taking blame and owning up to mistakes. Again, Ed Catmull in Creativity, Inc.: "If we as leaders can talk about our mistakes and our part in them, then we make it safe for others."[5]

Kids appreciate it when you own up to a mistake. It demonstrates your fallibility and humanity and gives the players an opportunity to support you for a change. It even allows for teachable moments in figuring out how it could have been done differently.

These mistakes are largely coaching or strategy errors: not recognizing the opponents' strength when play calling, not considering the other team's style of defense or offense—if they're playing zone defense or implementing a full-court press in basketball, not adjusting accordingly or quickly enough. That kind of decision falls squarely on the coach's shoulders. Or specifically, as is seared in my mind, when I sent a runner from second base toward home on a base hit to the gap only to have her tagged out by a perfect throw and tag.

Sometimes there are errors of human judgment that coaches have to own up to. It may hurt, but it's the right thing to do, and the kids will be grateful.

One summer I was asked to help coach a team as a favor to a friend and their coaching staff. I ran some practices, and after games, we'd discuss some highlights. Not a big deal. Until they reached the middle of a big game in a critical tournament.

---

5   Catmull, 111.

It turned out that one of my friend's team's starting players had to leave and suit up for a playoff game in another sport. Dilemma time. If a player left the game for a noninjury reason, there would be negative consequences. What should my friend, the coach, do? The player was told to fake an injury.

As I watched it unfold, I had this terrible feeling in my stomach and couldn't help but think, "Oh boy, this is not a good idea." Regrettably, I didn't say anything to the head coach as I saw it going down. This wasn't a coach trying the old hidden ball trick to fool another team. This was a coach having a player lie to an official. After the game, I discussed the issue with my friend, and we agreed that it was wrong.

There were a number of misfires here. The kid shouldn't have suited up in the first place. My friend shouldn't have let that player onto the field. I should have recommended a better approach. But ultimately, the coach made a terrible error in judgment and cheated … and the team knew it. This needed to be addressed head on immediately, or it would set a bad example that the kids would look to as guidance.

Errors, whether they come from a player or coach, are opportunities to build team support. Even the ones that are from bad judgment. And that's exactly what had happened with my friend. It was hard to do, especially as the team leader, but the coach addressed the team and admitted the lapse in judgment. It got a little emotional for the coach, and the players immediately rallied in support. It was a great moment for the team: the coach owned up to a big mistake, showed regret, and asked for their support. The team became much closer as a result.

Pick Your Moments

If you're going to let your players play and make mistakes, you're also going to have to know when to shut up. Yelling out instructions from the sideline is great for a micromanager … and really bad for anyone who wants the kids learning and thinking for themselves.

Let go of that impulse. You worked on fundamentals during practice. You set the plays up and worked on that during the week. Now it's game time. Trust that your kids paid attention and internalized the drills, the game plan, and your style of play. Now's your opportunity to get out of the way, be quiet, and encourage them to own what they're doing.

If you're running up and down the sidelines, yelling where the kids should pass the ball, which side they should go down, and where each player should be, you're not helping them increase their game IQ. You're trying to control them like puppets on a string. They'll be focused on carrying out your instructions instead of thinking for themselves.

What you should be doing is making sure the kids are acting and reacting in the moment. Let them work through the game, and give them support. Pick and choose what you call out to them. I'm not saying that you should be silent. If you stop by and watch me coach a game, I'm far from quiet. I'm animated, and I can get loud depending on the situation. I try to give feedback or ask a player what we could have done differently. What you won't hear from me is instruction on how to fix the fundamentals. I leave that for practice. Game day is about strategy, execution, and focusing on making plays.

Game day is exciting and stressful. Kids have enough on their minds without coaches (and parents) shouting out instructions to them. When a kid enters the batter's box, they should be thinking about their pitch count progression and hitting the ball. What they should *not* be thinking about is the many different voices from the dugout and the stands alternatively yelling, "Choke up!"

"Get that back elbow up!"

"Keep your head down!"

"Bend your knees!" And on and on and on.

Stop.

Get out of their way.

Trust that they'll focus on finding open space, passing to an open teammate, or getting the right pitch to swing at, and give them the best chance to succeed (or fail) on their own terms.

Will they make mistakes? Of course. And then that gives you something to discuss with the team in the postgame wrap-up to help everybody learn and maybe work on during the next practice.

After games, have a team huddle. Point out some things that went right, some things that went wrong. And then at the next practice, your players will have a bit more objectivity. As we talked about last chapter with creating a precise practice plan, start it with a debrief, and go over all those plays that weren't executed as planned, or cover new strategies used against your squad. Incorporate those into the day's agenda.

Remember: practices are for fundamentals and coaching. Games are for letting your players play.

Recognize That Some Days Just Ain't Your Days!

In February 2008 the New England Patriots were the runaway favorite for Super Bowl XLII. The club was thought of as one of the greatest teams in NFL history, having gone undefeated in the regular season and rolling through the playoffs. And … they just didn't have it that Super Bowl Sunday, losing 17–14 to the New York Giants in one of the biggest upsets not just in football but in any pro sport. The best team didn't play their best in that game. It just wasn't their day.

If it happens to pro athletes, it can happen to kids. Sometimes you can play your butts off and try to execute everything you've worked on, but it just doesn't happen. You know those games I'm talking about when no matter what the players do, it kind of falls flat. You look up at the scoreboard, and all of a sudden you're down eight runs or five goals. Nothing seems to go right, and all the luck appears to go one way (clearly, not yours).

Try to catch yourself before you react. Instead of throwing a fit during the game (or after), it's your turn to take a deep breath. Keep your players focused on the task at hand. The kids know how poorly they're doing; they don't need you (or their parents) to rub it in. In fact, if you take a step back, you can even have a laugh over it. It sucks while it's happening, but hey, sometimes it's not your day. What can you do?

Focus on what you and your players can control: their effort, their attitude, and the team-first, fearless environment. In the end, you still may end up on the wrong end of a lopsided loss, but if you are successful in keeping them focused, you'll see a group of players holding each other accountable and supporting each other. It'll keep the mood light and the atmosphere positive. That's what keeps teams in games and keeps players showing up to practice: having fun and improving throughout the season.

In 2014 I coached a 10U softball team, the Ninja Nightcrawlers. Our team was talented and very aggressive. On offense, we stole a lot of bases, executed hit and runs, and always tried to stretch singles into extra base hits. We had great pitching, a good defense, and strong catchers. One of the benefits of this type of team was that we would often challenge our catchers to look to pick off runners at first and third. My starting backstop one game was Grace, one of the most aggressive players I've ever coached. As the saying goes, her uniform was dirty before she left the dugout. She would dive, fight for the extra base, and at catcher, would love to try to pick off base runners!

About one-third of the way into the season, we were playing one of the better teams in our league, and we were tied in the bottom of the fifth, the next-to-last inning. Grace wanted to throw down to third after a pitch to pick off the runner. She signaled to me, and I gave her the green light. After the next pitch, Grace leaped up, had the runner dead to rights—and airmailed a throw five feet over the third baseman's stretched arm, letting the runner jog home to score.

Grace immediately felt terrible. But instead of bemoaning the play or cursing that we were now down a run, I jumped up, pointed to Grace, and loudly applauded her aggressive play. After the inning ended and the team came in, I reiterated how much I loved the drive behind that play. I added that it may not have worked out in that situation but that we would absolutely do it again in the same situation. The kids didn't let the play grind them down; they rallied, and we won the game.

In the postgame meeting, I repeated that our style of play will sometimes cost us but that we'll support our teammates when we fail, continue to go for it, and never back down. Grinning after a hard-fought win, they all agreed. That game and chain of events was a key moment in our season. Grace felt empowered to continue to be her aggressive self, and just as important, it sent a message to the team that we'd focus on attempting plays that other teams wouldn't even try. The kids ran with it—we didn't lose another game that season and finished league champions.

KEY COACHING POINTS

- **Create a supportive environment** that allows kids to make mistakes. Failure can be productive!
- **Get buy-in from coaches and parents** on allowing mistakes. It will redouble the kids' feeling of freedom.
- **Trust that what happened in practice will carry over to games.**

COACHING MISTAKES

- **Correcting player fundamentals in the middle of the game.** They have too many things to concentrate on beyond the micromanagement of their eyes, feet, and hands.
- **Yelling at a kid for a mistake.** It makes the player not want to screw up and gives others the license to yell.

TRANSFERABLE CAREER SKILL

- **Give employees and coworkers permission to fail.** Give them the leeway to learn through mistakes, and they'll learn it better, be more proactive, and be more creative.

CHAPTER SEVEN

"COACHING" YOUR TEAM'S PARENTS

> Leadership is a matter of having people
> look at you and gain confidence ... If
> you're in control, they're in control.
>
> **—Tom Landry**

In 2017 our All-Star softball team was playing in a pivotal game of our district tournament. We had carefully cultivated a team-first culture all year, and all the parents had given me their word that they'd abide by our team philosophy. One of the core rules of the supportive environment is that in the stands, parents just cheer and stay positive. When it's game time, the last thing players need are distracting orders. Up until this particular game, the entire season had been free of that.

All of a sudden two dads in the stands couldn't help themselves. "Move your hands back! Check your feet! Keep your head down!" I was livid. As the game got more intense, they got louder and louder, destroying our special atmosphere that the coaches and parents had worked so hard to build up for the kids. We had one of those games where we didn't play our best, and our opponent took advantage of it. We ended up blowing a 5–0 lead and lost the game. We were now faced with having to win three more games in the loser's bracket just to stay alive.

Immediately after the game, I took the two dads aside, and—well, let's just say that it got a little heated. I accused them of reneging on the deal we made at the top of the season and renewed at midyear. In the most crucial game of the season, I was only able to hear them, not my assistant coaches. The kids were distracted by their constant instructions and weren't able to focus. I reminded them what we had talked about all year, that it takes a village to build the environment that breeds success and that they had gone against everything we worked for. They were both silent. They may have been embarrassed or more likely pissed, but they heard me.

Our team was disappointed with the tough loss and the hole we'd dug ourselves into, but we were able to refocus and thrive in the loser's bracket. We knocked off the next three opponents by a combined score of 43–8. As fate would have it, we played the same team in the semifinals later in the tournament. They came out and built a 5–0 by the end of the first inning but not a single parent opened his or her mouth except to cheer. And what happened? We scored nine unanswered runs to knock them off and then took the next two games to win the district championship in dramatic fashion.

Up to this point, I've spent a lot of time talking around parents. I've talked extensively about the kids and the other coaches, but parents are a huge part of the village, and it's important to get buy-in from them as much as anybody else to build a team-first environment.

After all, it starts at home. For a kid to bring a great attitude to practice and games, it has to start with the parents. The parents can help their children put things in perspective, they can show excitement for the team and the coach, and put the kids in a positive frame of mind to compete and have fun.

Unfortunately, not all parents have good habits and behaviors when it comes to youth sports. Throughout my many years of coaching, I've found that as long as you're organized, have a program that is rooted in the four pillars, and address expectations and behavior, the parents will normally give you their support.

Most parents I've dealt with over my years of coaching have the best intentions when it comes to their children and their involvement in sports. Unfortunately, even good parents can behave in a manner detrimental to the environment you're trying to cultivate.

Be on the lookout for the following behaviors that can detract from the team-first environment:

- **Bleacher coaching.** Barking out lessons from the stands undermines the coaching staff and can confuse the kid. It doesn't matter who the instructions are aimed toward or if they came from an accomplished athlete; it doesn't fit on a team that's striving for unity, positivity, and trust.
- **Yelling/berating.** How many viral videos have you seen of youth sports parents losing it and coming to blows with one another? This is the gateway to that. Screaming at officials over close calls is bad enough; but hearing parents scream at kids over mistakes is awful and embarrassing. This kind of behavior is counterproductive to the supportive environment, and it makes the whole day uncomfortable for the

entire village.

- **Criticizing.** While yelling can ruin the program vocally and directly, criticism is more insidious, creating negativity and giving license to other parents to complain about the coaching, the team play, and even the kids. Loud criticism undermines the game strategy and teaching and can even bleed into insulting the other kids playing.

- **Helicoptering.** It's one thing to check in on a kid's welfare. It's another to constantly badger the coach to give a kid more playing time, an opportunity at another position, more favorable treatment, and on and on. Everybody in the village has a role. Trust that the coaches are developing a child on the team in the right way. If there are questions, conversations with the coaches are always welcome—but not in the middle of a game.

- **Not showing up.** As I said, everybody in the village has a role. The parents' role is to show up, smile, and be positive. Being absent or being distracted or inattentive at the field can have a negative effect on kids that will last long after the game is over. Be present. It's one of the easiest gifts you can give your budding athlete.

It's not a question of if but rather when and how often you'll encounter one or more of these behaviors. It's critical to address expected behavior up front with the parents. It's also critical that you address any detrimental behavior as quickly as possible after it occurs. If you allow it to go on (i.e., through multiple games), it will open the door for other parents to do the same. When this happens, the parent's kid is not the only one impacted; it affects the entire team. You can have a coaching staff that is completely aligned, but if you didn't do the groundwork with the parents, it won't matter.

So how can you coach a parent on how to tamp down bad behavior, be supportive, help create the environment for their kids, and remain a positive influence throughout the entire season?

- **Get buy-in at the first meeting.**
- **Explain the program and the expectations.**
- **Outline the parents' role.**
- **Check in (and recommit) at midseason.**

All this establishes and strengthens your relationship with the parents. When you make it clear that you're welcoming them as part of the village and the program to improve their kid and provide a good youth sports experience, they'll understand that you have a plan in place.

Get Buy-In at the First Meeting

Early in my coaching career, I made a big mistake. I basically ignored the parents. I wasn't able to see the role they'd play over the course of the season, so I made little effort to connect and explain my approach. As a result, I ended up in some acrimonious situations with a couple of parents. Eventually, I became so burned out from dealing with these problem parents that I briefly retired from coaching.

Much of this could have been prevented if I had had dialogue with the parents at the beginning, explained my philosophy, and established codes of conduct. That's exactly what I do now and what I strongly advise any coach to do. This won't eliminate detrimental behavior from parents, but it will help minimize it, making the entire team's season that much more enjoyable.

When a kid joins your team, you're not only coaching them, you're taking on their whole family. Parents play an integral role and need to support their children and the team by following the basic rules of conduct. I make a point of sitting down with parents just before or after the first practice in the same way I do with coaches and players.

In about half an hour, I'm able to give an overview of my coaching philosophy (see below) and describe the environment we're going to create. Like the kids, parents can sense disorganization and can act badly absent any parameters or trust in the fact that somebody's in charge. I come prepared with handouts—tailored for age and level of play—and give them the overview of my approach, walk them through what's expected of their kid, and what's expected of them. Being organized and confident will set many of the parents at ease. I'll run down my list of good behaviors and then get into examples of bad behavior. I try to keep it light and poke some fun at some of the more egregious bad behaviors I've encountered. This can get a chuckle, but at the same time, it sends a message that this type of behavior is not unique to this team or league, and it's destructive to the goals that we want for our team.

> Parents can sense disorganization and can act badly absent any parameters or trust in the fact that somebody's in charge.

Explain to the parents that not every kid will play their favorite position or play it for as long as they want. There are some kids who are, frankly, just going to be role players: pinch runners, third-quarter defenders, or backup guards in case starters need a break, foul out, or get injured. This has to be clearly explained at the outset. No parent wants to believe it's going to be their kid who'll end up sitting. That's why you have to be direct with them. On more competitive teams, I often find myself telling parents that while their kid may not play much, I guarantee they'll feel like a part of the team and will most certainly improve. Nine times out of ten, those parents will be great with that.

If you want everyone rowing in the same direction, you need alignment and agreement on the core tenets of the program. Set the tone with the parents, just as you do with the kids and coaches, and get that buy-in. As we discussed last chapter, look every parent in the eye when asking them to commit to the village and to keeping the other parents accountable. This physical and verbal assent means a lot. It gives you license to intervene when you see them crossing the line, it gives other parents that responsibility as well, and it sets the expectations for everyone involved. After all, it takes a village.

Explain the Program and the Expectations

There are certain points you'll want to hit on in that first meeting. They'll proactively answer many of the questions the parents may have and present you as organized, clear, and disciplined.

- **Who are you?** Describe your leadership style, why you love coaching, and what your background is. For me, I talk about the successes and failures I've had through undefeated and unvictorious teams and how they've helped form my coaching philosophy. I talk about building relationships with their kids and how I'll work with them over the course of the season.

- **Why are we here?** What's the purpose of this upcoming season? I talk about building a great experience that has the kids looking forward to the next year. I hammer home that we're here to teach the kids to be good people through sports, to create a safe environment for them to be challenged in. They'll challenge themselves and their teammates, occasionally fail and grow from their mistakes, and learn about the game and what it means to be a great teammate. All these things contribute to the team's success and their own.

- **What's your coaching philosophy?** I discuss the supportive, team-first environment I want to build for each kid. I talk about the four pillars, finding roles for every player no matter their skill level; and how playing time will be parceled out. This is the time I reiterate how crucial it is to let kids make mistakes. It may be difficult for some parents to hear and appreciate, but it's a key point to repeat.

- **What do we focus on?** These are the goals for the season. For me, it's my four pillars from chapter 1: building players' fundamentals, strengthening their game IQ, elevating teamwork, and having fun. Talk to the parents about the other team goals that you, the coaching staff, and the kids have come up with. Remind them that it takes time to develop all these skills, and reiterate that they need to be patient. Even talented teams still have areas to develop.

- **What do we *not* focus on?** Like the lesson of letting kids make mistakes, this is something to sear into the parents' minds. We don't care about wins and losses, championship banners, or (for the older kids) scholarships. If these result from our approach, that's fantastic. However, the process— teaching the kids to be better people through hard work and team-oriented behavior—is everything. Wins are a by-product of our program.

Being clear about your strategy and goals will help put the season and expectations for their kids in a sharp framework for the parents and help them understand what youth sports are about. We're not here to win a championship at the cost of all else. We're here to teach the kids how to develop attributes that will serve them well in sports and life: grit, courage, determination, confidence, self-control, self-lessness, sportsmanship, and passion.

That said, the meeting shouldn't be about berating them or cowing them into submission. After presenting the coaching philoso-phy, season overview, and what you expect out of their kids, move on to how they fit into the equation and how integral their role is in creating the environment and a positive experience for their children.

Bring them into the village by teaching them some of the common terms that the coaches and players will toss around. Vocab-ulary specific to each sport such as "Through the bag" or "Down!" for base runners in baseball. "Switch the field" and "Man on!" in soccer. It's good for the parents to know the terms so they can under-stand what's being said at games and so they can have positive, more informed interactions about the sport with their kids.

The season should be a two-way street of communication. Encourage feedback from parents (though not from the stands!). I make sure to let the parents know that I'm not perfect. Much like the kids, I will make mistakes as well, and if they have any suggestions or concerns, it's important they come to me. Complaining and negativ-ity can be detrimental to the team, so they should know that your door (or inbox) is always open. It takes a village to help grow kids into confident and noble young women and men. For our season, it's one team, one approach, and one mindset.

Outline the Parents' Role

In March 2018 a video of Frank Martin, the South Carolina Gamecocks men's basketball coach, went viral. It took place at a press conference where Martin discussed his son's fifth-grade basketball games and the bad behavior of so many kids' parents at youth games. Martin led off his diatribe with "I'm probably the most animated coach that you've probably ever seen when my team's playing. I go watch my kids play, I don't say boo. I don't wave my arms, I don't try to coach my kids."[6]

If a coach of that caliber understands the distinction between being a coach on the field and a parent in the stands, everyone should. If you could boil down what I ask of parents, it comes down to "be supportive, and be positive."

There are four main pieces of advice I give:

- **Let the coaches coach.**
- **Leave the officials alone.**
- **Support the kids and the team environment.**
- **Police yourselves.**

> Try to keep parents being parents. They're not the coaches, they're not the officials, and they're not the kids.

See a common thread there? Try to keep parents being parents. They're not the coaches, they're not the officials, and they're not the kids. Their job is to be positive and to create the atmosphere for their children at home. They get their kids in the

6   Morgan Moriarty, "South Carolina's Frank Martin Drops the Hammer …," SBNation, March 18, 2018, accessed February 1, 2019, https://www.sbnation.com/college-basketball/2018/3/18/17136604/frank-martin-south-carolina-parents-youth-sports.

right mindset, help them set expectations, support and encourage them, and remind them to be part of the team.

- **Let the coaches coach.** As Frank Martin says, sit in the stands and don't say boo. I'm a good coach, but when I watch my kids, I'm there as a parent. I'm not there to give instructions. The coaches have been assisting the kids for months—maybe years—and know what they're working on, on the court or diamond, field or rink. When your son or daughter is at the free throw line or lining up to take a corner kick, their head needs to be clear of outside voices so they can concentrate solely on the task at hand and what we've worked on in practice. Parents should be cheering or quietly enjoying the game.

- **Leave the officials alone.** It's funny—and also depressing— to see how many videos exist of irate parents storming the field at their third grader's soccer game to get into the ref's face. Do parents really think a referee, who's making maybe twenty or thirty bucks on a Sunday morning officiating for a bunch of nine-year-olds, woke up thinking, "How can I screw that kid Timmy's team today?" Sure, for parents who are emotionally wrapped up in their sons' and daughters' athletic endeavors, in the heat of the moment, it can feel that way. But refs are just like you and me. They're doing their best, and they're making the calls. Again, the most important thing is growing these children into well-rounded, strong adults. Whether or not every call on the soccer pitch went their way is not the point. How they're playing and how they're improving is.

  In the same way the coaching staff knows that there's somebody appointed to talk to the officials, parents should as well. A tough call that goes against your team shouldn't be addressed by a whining outcry. It should be handled by one of the coaches who can calmly discuss the call with the official. Another official may be brought in to continue the conversation, and whatever they determine is the final decision. In all my years of coaching, I can guarantee you that an uproar from the stands won't change their mind, and it certainly won't make them more likely to pull a close call for you the next time.

Another word to the wise for parents. There's no instant replay in youth sports. Everybody has a video camera in their pocket now. And with constant videoing of our kids, every sports parent has a camera angle on that last play that shows their son safe at second or their daughter fouled under the rim. Under no circumstances should a parent run up at a time-out or during halftime or after the game to thrust a phone into the official's face to prove them wrong.

- **Support the kids and the team environment.** As we discussed last chapter, there's so much fear around mistakes in schools, in sports, and all aspects of a kid's life. Tell the parents how good it is for their children's growth and confidence to let them make mistakes on the field. They'll grow from them, and so will their teammates.

  Encourage the parents to just cheer and smile. Challenge them to swallow any comments they have when their kid makes a mistake. When their kid gives the ball away, doesn't cover their man, strikes out looking, lets in a bad goal, or misses an open shot, just cheer and smile.

- **Police yourselves.** We all hold each other accountable in this village. The kids and other coaches hold me accountable;

teammates hold each other accountable. And parents have to hold one another accountable. If somebody is sniping from the stands, it's on other parents to put a stop to it. I can't be everywhere at once, and neither can you. This first meeting, setting up what's expected of them, allows you to reel them back when they step over the line and also enables other parents to remind each other what they agreed on.

Being a parent before, during, and after the game can be just as stressful as any other role. Giving them directives on how to behave could help them, and it will definitely help the team. Here's what I tell my parents:

- **Pregame.** Don't badger your daughter or son. Encourage them to play hard and have fun. Help them get into the mindset of being present and part of a team. Quietly remind yourself why they play youth sports … to have fun.

- **During the game.** The single best thing parents can do during games is cheer from the stands and offer unqualified support for their kids.

- **Postgame.** As a parent and kid walk away from the game and get in the car, I wonder if the parent's good behavior is continuing. Once the coach is out sight and out of mind, the mom or dad could just be picking the kid apart. That's a huge mistake. The player knows what they did wrong. We probably already talked about it, and we may cover it at the next practice. Let the coach do the coaching. Parents should stay positive; let the child know it was fun watching them play, period. If I could give the parents on my team one piece of advice, it would be "Let them know that you love them and your love does not depend on their athletic performance." You'd be amazed how far that goes.

Check In (and Recommit) at Midseason

I've found that attention to our commitment and agreement can wane over the course of a long season. Bad behavior has the tendency to creep in. Check in with parents around midseason to make sure everyone is still committed to staying supportive and positive, knowing what lane they're driving in, and bolstering the team environment.

I sometimes call a midseason meeting or send emails to parents to update them on players' development and remind them of their roles and responsibilities. Reconnect with the parents as a group, and ask for their pledge again as you tackle the second half of the season. It's also handy to let them know you still value their feedback.

The midseason check-in also primes parents for playoffs. As the weeks wind down and the intensity going into the postseason ratchets up, that's when the coaching staff has to make those hard decisions: remind the parents that some kids will be playing less, and there will be less rotating through positions.

OTHER ROLES FOR PARENTS

The longer you're in a league, the more you'll begin to recognize the parents who won't be a good fit on your coaching staff and the more you'll want to guard yourself against them if they want to be a part of it. It's okay to decline their help. Better to be straight with them instead of getting into a situation with a hothead coach who upends your positive environment. It'll save time and energy if you cut that off at the pass.

Luckily, head coaches often know the team rosters before the parents and kids do. When I can, I do some research into the families on my roster and try to set my staff in advance. If problem parents then ask to be an assistant, I'm able to let them down easy and explain that we're all set for the season.

It's crucial, however, that you don't burn bridges. Parents play a key role in the village. If parents want a role in a noncoaching capacity, find a way for them to help that doesn't involve field time. Parents can take care of administrative things such as registering the team for a tournament, coordinating snacks for the games, or fundraising. They can take on the role of "Team Parent" and run the team page through third-party websites such as Shutterfly, where they can post pictures, list accomplishments, and handle scheduling.

As always, if you don't have enough information about certain parents, ask around. Networking can make sure you avoid problems. Be confident and firm, and trust your decisions.

Being up front about the team philosophy and how you work with the players builds a sense of trust between you and the parents. Telling them how your coaching strategy will develop their child as a player, teammate, and person is really what every parent should want out of youth sports. That growth is the goal. Any celebratory accomplishments on the field are basically icing on the cake. And when they do come, they're all the sweeter.

Our 2017 14U All-Star girls' softball team had a core of nine starters, with room on our roster to take on a couple more kids. We decided to add two kids who had never played on an All-Star team. Both Haley and Emily worked hard and brought positive attitudes to the field every day. It also didn't hurt that we really liked their parents, who were all supportive and positive. Before the selections were finalized, I met with both sets of parents separately, and I was blunt. I told them that we were considering their girls for the team.

There was a chance that they would only be role players and not get any playing time. However, I promised that they'd be and feel a part of the team and would absolutely improve by practicing at a very high level.

The parents were not only fine with zero expectations of playing time, they were thrilled that their girls had this incredible opportunity. Paul (a coach as well), Debbie, Jeff, and Kim were all great parents that got it. They were excellent contributors to our village.

While they may have been role players, Haley and Emily made the most of opportunities to step in for the regulars. When one of our starters was unavailable for our final tune-up tournament before our district championships, Haley was inserted into the lineup. In the final game, she recorded seven outs at third base, including the final two to seal the tournament championship at 5–0.

In the district championship game, both of our starting pitchers were gassed after playing in back-to-back games in the ninety-degree weather. Emily hadn't pitched in a few weeks, but we needed her to step in. I handed her the ball and asked her to give us two innings. She calmly trotted onto the field (with her dad, Paul, quietly freaking out in the stands) and pitched a gem as we ended up winning the game in extra innings.

These wins were great, but seeing these girls' confidence walking off the field and seeing their parents beaming with pride was even better. Both Haley and Emily contributed to our success that season. They had incredible moments individually as players, but more importantly, they were part of a team experience that they'll remember for the rest of their lives. None of it would have happened without the positive support of their parents.

Great parents combined with clearly communicated expectations lead to amazing results.

KEY COACHING POINTS

- **Setting the tone up front** is everything. Be as detailed as possible on the team philosophy and big picture of the season. Specificity and organization can help parents trust you and lean into their roles.
- **Get buy-in from the parents** to hold them accountable if lines are crossed.

COACHING MISTAKES

- **Ignoring the parents' role and your relationships** with them. All participants are critical to the team's ultimate success.
- **Letting parents' bad behaviors metastasize** and avoiding the problems. If you see a line being crossed, address it immediately.

TRANSFERABLE CAREER SKILL

- **Being detailed during meetings.** Whether you're running a department or a meeting, specificity and a disciplined tone are crucial.
- **Buy-in makes coworkers feel like a bigger part of the company and program.** When people have a role, they feel more involved and responsible.

CHAPTER EIGHT

COACHING YOUR OWN CHILDREN

Praise your kids. Inspire and motivate your players with praise. Ten years from now it won't matter what your record was. Will your kids love or hate you?

—Jim Harrick

The rewards of coaching are priceless, but coaching kids, especially your own, can also be difficult. The environment we work in is always changing, and that brings new challenges every year. Sometimes we forget the real reasons kids play sports or why we're out there in the first place.

If you're reading this, I'd bet that you have a kid who plays a sport, very likely on a team you coach or are thinking about coaching. The fact is the majority of coaches have kids on the team. That's normally how it goes. But as the village chief, you'll likely have players who look up to you as a parental figure. Let's look more at these dynamics and how to approach them successfully:

- **your kid as your player and**
- **your player as your kid.**

Your Kid as Your Player

Coaching your own kid(s) can be so rewarding—watching them improve athletically and socially while bonding with teammates through the ups and downs of a season. Yet some difficult situations can emerge in a setting where the parent is the coach and authority figure. Navigating the relationship from parent-child to coach-player can be tricky. You know your child and the way they behave (and misbehave) intimately well, and they're uniquely able to push your buttons. There are common pitfalls you want to avoid when coaching your own kid. It may all sound intuitive, but it's worth going over.

Favoritism, nepotism, whatever you want to call it—it's real, and it sucks. Daddy Ball, which we discussed in chapter 4, is that nefarious way coaches give preferential treatment to their kid, in the form of more playing time, more time at key positions, or pushing their own kid on All-Star teams when the kid is undeserving of the honor. It's mind boggling to me. It hurts the team, is disrespectful to more deserving players, and is counterproductive to their own kid, who might be playing way out of his league.

Treating your child with, well, kid gloves on her sports team doesn't build character, and it's not good for either of you. At the same time, being harder on your kids because you expect more out of them, you want them to improve more, or you're taking something from home out on them on the field—those are terrible ideas as well.

These girls and boys and their teammates don't need to be reminded that you're their parent. Don't treat them differently than you would the other kids.

For me, I was so concerned about the perception of being a Daddy Ball coach that I swung too far the other way. I was much tougher on my kids and almost wore that like a badge of honor. It was the wrong thing to do, and if I could change one thing in coaching my kids in the early years, I would've just treated them as I did the others.

At the same time, you can't allow your kid—and this'll be harder when they're young—to put you in a position where you're parenting them on the field. Because you have a deep and complex relationship with your own child, bad behavior can sometimes pop out that normally wouldn't. Your kid wouldn't be having this temper tantrum with another coach, and you wouldn't be yelling at another player the way you did at your own child.

When my son, Tyler, was playing soccer with the U10 Electric Thunder Chickens, we were once in the middle of a game where I had him playing the midfield. Tyler was one of the more talented players on our roster, but as a nine-year-old, he was also one of the younger players. There were several games where he took over the game and helped his team pull together a win. He would often draw multiple defenders to him, and he was (and still is) very good at seeing the entire field. He would create opportunities throughout the game for his teammates to score by feeding them the ball after drawing the defenders out. If the defenders didn't jump out, he would bury it himself. It was a lot of fun to have this kid as a weapon for my team, and it was exciting, as his dad, to see him leading.

In this particular game, Tyler seemed to be just going through the motions. He was running around but clearly not putting in a max effort as nine-year-olds will sometimes do. This annoys me as a coach and a dad. So I started to let him have it. I was stalking up and down the sidelines, barking at him to get moving. And then he started going slower. I was about to lose my top when my buddy Dan pulled me over and said, "Dude, calm down. What are you doing?" I was totally mortified. I was acting like all those ass-backward coaches who think that shouting yields results.

So there we were. I was losing it with Tyler, and in the story that opened this book, Krista was thinking about walking away from softball. My overcharged coaching of my kids was affecting them both.

> How could I recover our relationship, and how could I keep her on the team?

When Krista told me she was thinking about not playing All-Star softball, it was a turning point for me. How could I recover our relationship, and how could I keep her on the team? Something was going to suffer, perhaps irreversibly, if I couldn't change course. It wasn't only that I wanted her to be a part of the team as it took that next step of growth, but I loved spending time with her while driving to games, going to tournaments, and hanging out in hotel rooms. It was a special bond we had, and it was in danger.

The first thing I did was have a conversation with her. We talked, and I apologized, saying, "I'm sorry I treated you differently than the other players." I explained that it was my fault, and I was going to make some changes. I also told her that she deserved to be treated just like any other kid on the team, positively and constructively. I did the same with Tyler.

Krista signed up to play All-Stars another year, thankfully, though I was aware things had to change on the field. By this point in our relationship, both in the parent-kid and coach-player realms, she knew what would get my goat. If she didn't block a ball behind the plate or if she didn't throw with her elbow up, she knew I'd always be there to point it out. But when the season rolled around and Krista was playing and every now and then making those kinds of fundamental errors, I didn't say anything. She sent me a confused look, like the dog whose owner has put down two dinner bowls. Like, "I'm not gonna complain, but what's the catch here?"

This was only part of the battle. The second ingredient toward a working relationship with my kids on the field and something that I advocate other parent-coaches learn is the fact that it really does take a village. I went to the other coaches and explained what was happening. "Guys," I said, "I'm failing." I talked about what was happening with me and Krista and told them that I needed their help. I asked them to step in when they saw something that needed to be corrected.

Perhaps unsurprisingly, each of them admitted to having the same problem. One talked about how he was walking on eggshells with his daughter, that whenever they came to the field, he absolutely got stonewalled. It turns out it was a common problem with a simple solution.

As with the complementary skill sets with coaches, we each were able to step in and take on the task of coaching and teaching each other's kids.

Doesn't this make sense? Our kids know just how to push our buttons in just the right ways. You can tell your kids to put on their coats seventeen times, and they'll ignore you every single time, but as soon as a grandparent or friend says it, zip. No problem. It's only natural to run into a little bit of that resistance every now and then on the field or court, but when the relationship between the parents and kids has more friction than usual, you can hit a roadblock as a coach.

All the coaches made a commitment to one another that if we hit a sensitive spot with our own kids on the field, another coach would step in. Coach Rob is a wonderful coach and has a great relationship with my kid. He knew exactly what to say or do to get her to smile (not an easy task) and then do what he asked her to do, and I had the same relationship with his kid, Erin. So we all made the agreement. We'd help manage each other's kids throughout the entire season … every single practice, warm-up, and game.

It can be incredibly rewarding coaching your kids, especially as you see the products of hard work and teamwork on the sports fields start paying off in other areas of their lives. It may sound silly, but I take a certain amount of pride listening to Tyler when plays those massive multiplayer online video games. He's got his headset on, and I swear, it's like he's handing out directions on the soccer field. Even if the leadership role he's assumed on the soccer pitch has bled over to nothing more than telling some friends and other teenagers in Oklahoma and Pennsylvania what route to run to attack another team, he's still the one in charge, seeing the field and figuring out the play.

When those flashes of maturity and leadership come out on the playing field, that's even sweeter.

Our 2016 All-Star softball team was playing in the state semifinals, and the mercury hit triple digits. During the summer, the temperature can soar during softball games, and that can be tough on your catchers. Wearing all that equipment in one-hundred-degree weather? Not so fun.

We were fortunate enough to have two great catchers (Mya and my daughter, Krista). Mya caught the first two games that day and was spent, so Krista put on the gear for game three. In the third inning of a very close game, there was a play at home. Krista received the ball and dropped down to tag a sliding runner. I was thrilled to see her make a great play for the team, but then I realized that something was wrong. Krista was still sitting there staring at her hand. She had jammed her thumb, bending her nail painfully back. We were screwed.

Rick Mack, another key coach that I had worked with for several years, jumped into action. Coach Rick was our jack-of-all-trades coach, and with over thirty years as a fireman, he knew it was one of his roles to evaluate the severity of injuries. He asked Krista if she wanted to come out of the game. She said that she could play, but her bleeding thumb told a different story. I was just about to tell Mya to suit up when my daughter calmly said, "Mya can't play. I have to catch. Tape me up, and I'm staying in." I couldn't have been prouder as a coach and parent.

Your Player as Your Kid

In addition to your own son or daughter, there'll be a lot of kids who look at you as a surrogate parent at times. They're not your biological children, but you begin to take on a father or mother role with them, as they may be looking for a strong adult figure in their lives for whatever reason. Maybe they're dealing with personal issues at home or are at a vulnerable point in their lives and need a good role model to help them navigate something difficult.

Or maybe they just like the structure and discipline that an older authority figure provides for them … as long as it's not their own parent! And here you are, doing something cool like coaching a sport they're into and connecting with them personally every week. You also may be a constant in the child's life from year to year. It's totally natural that kids may gravitate toward you for emotional support, even if they don't know they're doing it.

Players who are referred to as "problem children" may be dealing with an awful lot that's not immediately apparent: a divorce, an absentee parent, or a death in the family. It makes sense that this stress could bleed into other areas of their lives and that their behavior at practice would be impacted. With boys or girls who are going through something difficult, it helps to take all that into account. It's important to remember that they're kids. Bringing an approach of understanding will likely go a long way for them and your relationship.

This doesn't mean you should be more lenient on them when it comes to actual coaching, but it helps to have empathy on your side and show a little tolerance. If kids are acting out and you know what might be at the root of it, you can pull them aside and speak with them on a deeper level. Show them understanding, but hold them accountable to what all the players agreed to at the beginning of the season: focusing on the team, being supportive of each other, and showing up to practices and games ready to play.

> Knowing when to parent, when to coach, and when to step aside on either is key to maintaining a relationship with your kids and other children on the playing field, wherever it is.

Knowing when to parent, when to coach, and when to step aside on either is key to maintaining a relationship with your kids and other children on the playing field, wherever it is. It's another great reason to have put together a complementary coaching staff whom you trust and can lean on when things get hairy with your own child as they inevitably will at some point. That's the kind of relationship I've had with my coaches and what I hope I've provided for them as well.

Coach Rob and his daughter, Erin, had a huge blowup right before the 2017 district quarterfinals. I don't remember where it came from or what it was about, but it was bad. We had a tough match on deck against the wipe-that-smile-off-your-face rival, the winner of which would clinch an automatic berth in the state championships.

After the fight, Erin, who was slated to be our starting pitcher for the upcoming game, stormed off, claiming that she wouldn't play. Based on what we'd been through and learned, Rob knew he wasn't the one who needed to talk to her. That responsibility would fall on me, just as it would be on Rob if my daughter were the one having the meltdown.

I took Erin to the side and said, "Hey, Grabes, I need you to pitch this game. We all need you to step out there and pitch your ass off."

She hesitated for a moment and then looked me right in the eyes and said, "Don't worry, Coach. I got this." In the top of the first inning, Erin was still working through some emotion and tension, and we gave up three runs. Though our rivals thought they had us on the ropes, Erin knew that her team and the coaching staff had her back. She quickly recovered, and we blanked them for the rest of the game. Erin and her teammates scored 16 unanswered runs for a lopsided 16–3 win. If Rob had been the only coach there that day, chances are that his daughter would not have played.

It's hard to keep family emotions out of the equation when you're on the field. Having other coaches step in makes it work.

KEY COACHING POINTS

- **Treat your kids like any other player.** Don't be harder on them, and don't go easier on them. There's enough attention on the player as the coach's kid as it is.
- **Know when to rely on other coaches** to help manage your kid as a player.

COACHING MISTAKES

- **Overworking your kid** and expecting more out of them. They're there to play just like any other team member. Don't bring outside emotions and baggage onto the field.

TRANSFERABLE CAREER SKILL

- **Treat all employees and coworkers the same** even if there's an external relationship there. Keep the professional, professional and the personal, personal.

CHAPTER NINE

HAVE FUN!

Just play. Have fun. Enjoy the game.

—Michael Jordan

In 2017 our 14U softball team was playing in the district championships and the mood was heavy. We had lost a tough game the day before, the one in which I had had to correct parents for bleacher coaching. With our backs against the wall, we then won a few games to advance into the final four. The only way we were going to walk away district champs was if we won four games straight starting that day, including two straight against the team that made it through the winner's bracket.

At this point, you know the story. We won the next two games and found ourselves in the championship, where we were facing a fantastic Torrance team. If we won the first game, we'd earn ourselves another game in the scorching summer heat for the title. The girls were feeling the tension. Torrance had had us in their crosshairs the entire season.

We'd beaten them during the 2016 All-Star season, but the girls from Torrance had put us on notice with a 12–1 beatdown in a preseason game. The table was set for an epic battle for the title, and neither team disappointed. The game started, and we quickly found ourselves down four runs. The intensity was mounting, and you could sense that our girls were beginning to show signs of fatigue. So what did we do? Go over outfield coverage scenarios? Analyze their pitcher? Up the intensity?

A funny dance and song, of course. While Coach Rick was cringing in the dugout, Coach Rob and I shimmied outside the dugout, chanting a common girls' softball dugout cheer: "Top of the lineup, top, top of the lineup!" The biggest game of the season and here were the coaches dancing around like clowns to lighten the mood. And it worked. The kids breathed and relaxed and came back to win the game in extra innings.

My coaching staff and I have often been asked how our players could be so successful yet also have so much fun during high-stakes games. The answer is simple, and it's another ingredient in the secret sauce of the program: encourage them to be themselves, and empower them to make decisions and take responsibility. We let them play. Our players had the freedom to bring their own quirky, fun personalities to the team. The girls ran the games; they constantly communicated, joked around, and did it all with smiles on their face while kicking some serious butt.

In chapter 6, we looked at how serious youth sports have become. All you have to do is wander around some kids' fields and courts to see that in action. Stern-looking coaches, kids anxious about making mistakes, not talking with teammates. It's like a job now—or worse, another class at school. On top of this, there are girls and boys pressured to choose just one sport at the age of eight. Instead of soccer in the fall, basketball in the winter, softball or lacrosse in the spring, so many children are devoting the whole calendar to just one sport.

When did it all get so serious, and how do we reverse this? Because it's a problem. Both for kids' enjoyment and education and also for their health. This isn't just my feeling: take the academic researcher's word for it.

In 2014 the Aspen Institute's Project Play released a study full of key recommendations for youth sports called Getting and Keeping Kids in the Game. The major goals they listed from medical and health groups were

1. increasing regular physical activity for all kids and maintaining an emphasis on fun,
2. discouraging early sports specialization and overuse/overload, and
3. recommending age-appropriate sports development with youth-development-specific coaching education.[7]

Sound about right?

Get rid of specialization.

Single-sport specialization amongst youth today is troubling. Let kids be kids. They'll become better all-around athletes and have more fun.

—J. J. Watt

Earlier and earlier, parents are mistakenly pushing their kids to focus on just one sport year round. That's a pretty great way to take

7   John O. Spengler, Getting and Keeping Kids in the Game, the Aspen Institute Project Play, February 2014, accessed February 23, 2018, https://assets.aspen-institute.org/content/uploads/files/content/upload/Consolidated_Recs_of_Health_Medical_Groups.pdf.

the fun out of the entire endeavor: force the kids to forget about all the other sports they enjoy in favor of just one when they're still in elementary school.

I constantly hear from the one-sport parents, "We don't want them to fall behind." This thought process is misguided for most kids. The majority of kids would prefer to play multiple sports, and most of the better players I've coached played more than one sport at least through the age of fourteen.

And it's not just about having fun by sampling other athletics. What the parents miss is the same thing your CrossFit trainer or physical therapist will tell you. Kids have to rotate the muscle work. Repetitive motion is a surefire path toward injury. Furthermore, "diversified sports training during early and middle adolescence may be more effective in developing elite-level skills in the primary sport due to skill transfer."[8]

Age-appropriate development and coaching. As I said, don't teach eight-year-olds the same fundamentals as fourteen-year-olds. Consider the children's physical and mental maturation to get proper training techniques down.

Finally, and most important for this chapter, maintain an emphasis on fun. It's why we're here in the first place! Kids want to have fun, and the parents and coaches want to spend quality time with them. It's not happening as often as it should. It's up to you to reverse that trend on your team.

Just like being organized and taking responsibility, kids learn that it's okay to have fun by watching the grown-ups in the room. That's you, the assistant coaches, and the parents. Encourage them all to take down the adult shields and loosen up. When the players see you having fun and setting the tone, they'll be able to relax.

---

8   Spengler, Getting and Keeping.

Let's take a look at how you set that tone in every aspect of your season:

- **fun in practice,**
- **fun in games,**
- **empowering the players,**
- **fun with players, and**
- **fun with coaches.**

Fun in Practice

Let's call it "fun with fundamentals." It's the approach of mixing a focus on fundamentals and precision in practice with a light heart and fun. We're going to play, but we're going to take it seriously.

It may be tough for some new coaches to fully accept this philosophy. Just like letting the kids make mistakes, allowing the adult shield to come down and having fun with the kids may run counter to how they've operated before. It's part of my job to set the tone and give them the green light to do it their own way.

The responsibility for running effective practices that ensure the kids are having a good time and giving it their all lands with the village chief. It's up to you to track that they're paying attention to the legwork, footwork, and arm work, and it's also up to you to let them be playful with it.

For example, if my kids in softball are doing throwing drills with one another, I want them to be mindful of their motions,

> The responsibility for running effective practices that ensure the kids are having a good time and giving it their all lands with the village chief.

but if a kid launches a ball four feet above her partner's head, I'm going to have a little fun with it. Maybe I'll make an exaggerated noise or raise my eyebrows and say, "Whaaaaaaaaat?" or make a lighthearted "Worst. Throw. Ever" comment. This lets the kids know that while they messed up, I'm not going to lose my temper or discipline them the way some coaches would. While one of the kids is running to retrieve the ball, maybe I'll jokingly kick dirt on the perpetrator's cleats. With a smile on my face, I then ask them two critical questions:

- What do you think went wrong?
- How could you have done it better, or how could you fix it?

And then they're back to it.

The fundamentals we're working on are the building blocks for growth as a player. You let them know why each drill is important and put it in the big picture of development. At the same time, we're keeping it light. Tension and a fear of screwing up doesn't allow kids to feel at ease and do their best work. Who would want to play with that kind of atmosphere? Constructing a safe environment loosens your players up and allows them to breathe into each exercise and do their best.

I keep the tone throughout practice wildly positive. A shortstop makes a perfect throw to first? I'll cheer the heck out of that. A midfielder finds his teammate in front of the goal and feeds him a perfect cross for an assist? I'll whoop and holler. That positivity helps keep the mood playful and supportive and congeal the team as a unit.

It's important to keep things moving quickly and keep the kids involved throughout practice. I like to pepper in competitive games that reinforce that day's fundamentals. The kids love the competition, and they're able to practice them at game speed.

Every now and then, a practice may go off the rails. Maybe somebody's goofing off and taking the playful atmosphere too far or the players are losing focus. No problem: I'll get deadly serious for a moment and remind the kids of the importance of the drills and scrimmages, the exact precision we need to have, and how that fits into our season goals. And then it's right back to it and having fun with them.

I also like incorporating players' creativity into a special part of practices. For a handful of minutes during drills, I let the kids do something goofy or inventive when it's their turn, just for kicks and to get their outside-of-the-box brain working. For example, in baseball or softball, let's say we're turning two. For one round of the drill, I let the players do something wild and fun when they get the ball. This often yields a barehanded grab, a backhanded diving toss to the bag, or a behind-the-back toss. Anything goes—the kids have fun, and I give them points for creativity and difficulty.

Another example comes from soccer. I set the kids thirty feet apart. One player passes to the opposite side, and the receiving player dribbles the ball into the "creative zone" (marked off with a couple of cones) and has to do something different, funky, and creative. Typically, in the first practice, the kids do something goofy or funny. But then incrementally, the kids will try something creative and also difficult, such as a crazy dance that turns into a pull back of the ball or a quick little set of spins. Now they're seeing the fun to be had and the lesson behind the drill.

> The fun and loose atmosphere can yield some pretty amazing, inventive results that bear fruit.

The amazing thing is that because the kids are enjoying themselves and relaxing, they brainstorm some excellent maneuvers. It's even cooler when one of your players tries one of these maneuvers during the game. That's when it clicks. The fun and loose atmosphere can yield some pretty amazing, inventive results that bear fruit.

Showing the kids this approach to practice and the balance of focus and humor sets the tone for the entire season. It's not long before the players have internalized those guideposts for themselves and they're joking with one another but giving their absolute concentration to drills.

Fun in Games

We keep this tone on game days. It's not like games come around and all of a sudden I ratchet up the intensity. We keep it fun. I'm on the sidelines, maintaining that aggressive positivity—cheering the great saves, goals, passes, hits, all of it. And during halftimes or between periods or innings, I'm keeping the tone light with the kids.

At the same time, it's also critical to keep them accountable to the guideposts and our game plan with communication during the game. I use the same goofy behavior above when errors happen and then ask those same two critical questions:

- What do you think went wrong?
- How could you have done it better, or how could you fix it?

And then they're back to it.

Remember, you've worked on all the drills and scenarios during practices. Game time is for the kids to take over and play their best. Mistakes will happen but so will those fantastic moments when the kids carry over a lesson from practice and implement it in the game. Turning two on the diamond or executing a complicated passing play. During the game, I'm keeping the kids on target, being supportive, and carefully choosing when and where to say something.

One other thing I do during games is take notes. Remember when I said "write your practice plan down" in chapter 5? It always helps to have your crib notes handy. Every game, I have the lineup, reminders, our written-out style of play, and our goals and KPIs neatly laid out on a piece of paper. I also leave space to keep notes for things I see during the game that accentuate what we've been working on. Heads-up plays, fun plays, plays of incredible skill. Sometimes it's the great save by the goalie or the steal and layup by a guard. But just as often it's a great pass back in soccer when the pressure was on; three perfect, quick passes to get us out of our zone; or our right fielder backing up a play at first base.

Or sometimes, it's just a funny play that keeps the team loose.

My daughter, Krista, was playing first base during another important game in the 2017 Western nationals. With two outs in the third inning, a high fly ball came her way. She called for it, cleared the area … then promptly tripped over her own feet, made the catch, and landed on her face.

All the players ran over to make sure she was okay. She popped up, spitting out dirt, with the biggest smile on her face. It ended the inning and good thing, too, because the team, including my daughter, erupted in laughter. It was an excellent moment of humor with a great play attached to it in this intense game. The coaches still refer to it with their players every now and then in the lesson "How Not to Catch a Fly Ball."

These are the kinds of plays I write down throughout the games and refer to during postgame team meetings, giving the kids positive feedback and a sense of unity. Depending on their age, that positivity doesn't end with just the good words at the team meeting. Like the Ohio State Buckeyes loading up their players' football helmets with decals as a reward for great play, I'm also a big fan of handing out stickers with our team logo on them. Whether it's hockey, lacrosse, softball or baseball, if there's a helmet, the players are getting stickers.

Soccer and basketball players get patches.

During the postgame team meetings, I first ask the kids to call out something awesome that they saw a teammate do during the game. This helps build camaraderie as they recognize the accomplishments of their teammates. Early in the season, the kids will point to the obvious things: T-Bone's great top-shelf goal or Slugger's opposite field dinger. As the season progresses, they begin to notice the smaller things as well, which shows how their game IQ is advancing. They know that I'll ask them after every game, so they're looking for those passes that create space for a teammate, that backside help, and those moments of good sportsmanship. They begin to see the entire field and the entire play. As a result, they're far more appreciative of the work all their teammates are doing and become even more unified as a team. Once the players have exhausted the list of awesome things they saw, I'll add anything they missed from my notes.

And guess what else? It's really cool to see other teams blown away when our players run out with decals all over their helmets. Team logos and sharp, customized uniforms have an impact beyond just group unity. Like Deion Sanders said, "If you look good, you feel good. If you feel good, you play good." Same as the decals. It's fun for the kids to wear them, and they impress and intimidate our opponents. Our kids and many of the parents enjoy wearing our unique Swamp Donkeys or Junkyard Bunnies or Raging Unicorns branded swag.

Empowering the Players

Legendary Yankees skipper Joe Torre had a tradition at the end of regular seasons, in which he let one of his players manage the game. I think that's a great way to empower your players, and I have similar traditions. Toward the end of the year in soccer, hockey, or basketball, I designate one kid each quarter to hold the clipboard and set the lineup. Same with the final week of baseball and softball. Instead of coaches going out to first and third base when we're hitting, I have the kids do it.

Like the kids' involvement in the postgame sticker awards, these are small actions in the scope of everything else, but they give the players an even more heightened sense of responsibility. The kids look at the game from a different perspective, taking more things into consideration than only their immediate position. These activities advance game IQ and put them in a leadership role. That's part of the program: helping develop and grow the kids as players and people.

Fun with Players

Team bonding exercises stretch beyond wearing the same (awesome) logo on clothing. That atmosphere of team-first culture stretches into how we celebrate with one another and how we act as a unit.

It's all about the relationships between coaches and players and among the teammates themselves. Nicknames play a huge role in sports, and youth sports is no different. Mayhem, T-Bone, TT Slider, Springs, the Cuke, Iron Head, Sniper, Tank, Smashley, Beast, Graber, Wheels, Sticks, Slugger, Bazooka, Big Game James—all those have found their way onto teams of mine. Any kind of riff on the kid's last name, like adding a Y to the end (e.g., Swartzy, Wadgey, etc.) is always a go-to. And then you've got those customized, unique ones that the kids love too. I had a quick player on my 2016 All-Star softball team whose last name was Cdebaca. Say it out loud, and you can guess how her name went from Cdebaca to Chewbacca before we settled on Chewy. The team loved it and so did she as she grinned when her teammates would yell in unison, "Come on, Chewy!" when she was at the plate.

I had a set of twins on a softball team once; one played first, and the other played outfield. When the first baseman got clobbered by an opposing runner in the base path, she suffered a bloody nose and was pretty dazed but didn't want to leave the game. Based on that hard-nosed style of play, she earned the nickname Nailz. Not that unique but we then started calling her twin sister Featherz as a joke, which also caught on.

These nicknames may seem trivial, but they're not. They create team unity, and they give each player an identity that's unique and special. Through that, the kids feel like they're part of something bigger, no matter the size of their roles on the team.

Those special handshakes you see in pro sports? Try them out with your players as well. High fives, knuckles, low fives in the dirt, fist bumps, special complicated slaps, and daps: all of it. Some of the players will have individualized rituals, like Graber, who would grab some dirt and rub it into my shoulder as a ritual before every game during the 2017 run. Mya would check in before each elimination game to make sure I was wearing my "elimination" socks and shorts. The point is connecting with the players, letting them be themselves, and having fun.

There's no shortage of fun team bonding rituals you can do with your team. Sometimes my players would dye their hair for playoffs, something that the kids loved and the parents hated. (Make sure you get parental approval first!) Or you could have war paint as extended eye black in cool patterns and stripes. I'm a big heavy metal fan, so the Mötley Crüe *Shout at the Devil* Tommy Lee with two swipes down his cheeks has a special place in my heart. Other players want cat whiskers; some want the team colors. Hey, go crazy with it!

My 2019 All-Star softball team had a ritual between games where the kids would play Wiffle ball with one of our coaches, Brad

Swartzlander. Coach Brad was a master of goofy, fun activities to keep the mood light between games or before practice. He also created a Wiffle ball home run derby where one player would hit while the others formed a wall. He was all cheerful exuberance when he pitched, acting like he had won the World Series when he got one of them out. Meanwhile Coach Chris would be egging them on, yelling, "Yeah baby!"

Have fun.

When I coached lacrosse, the kids were always in for a treat at the end of the season. I was a box lacrosse goalie growing up, so I would throw myself into the net during the final practice before the playoffs started. The kids would have a field day taking shots on the coach. They got a kick out of watching me make some difficult saves … and they were thrilled when they got one by me! It's another example of having fun with the kids while also making sure they're practicing.

These are again part of the lighthearted attitude, but they don't get in the way of our style of play and laser focus, either. Sure, we've got the great swag, the stylish handshakes, and the war paint, but we're still incredibly intent on the precision of our drills and giving it our all at game time. Our tone of fun with fundamentals stays the same.

Fun with Coaches

The relationships you're building on the team don't stop with the players. Like any workplace culture, you want to make sure everyone is getting along and trusting one another. That extends to the coaching staff. I've made a point of getting to know my coaches through team meetings, and those team meetings often end up in bars. Alcohol isn't a necessity; it's the social aspect of connecting with one another that's important. You want to collaborate on strategy and upcoming practices and check in on the players' progress, but you also want to learn a bit more about each other. As with the kids, find out what makes your assistant coaches tick. Share stories about your families and sports backgrounds, and you'll be surprised what you end up talking about and how you connect.

The more you get to know them, the more comfortable they'll feel about being loose and fun on the field. When all the coaches are relaxed and letting their adult shields down, they'll give the kids even more of that license to relax. And the more the coaching staff gets to know and trust each other, the more confident you'll be that they'll have your back on the field and the safer you'll feel in holding each other accountable.

Keep those kids and coaches having fun and learning. It'll keep them engaged with the team and sport and interested in returning week after week and year after year. Now back to the Aspen Institute's Project Play:

"Fewer than 1 percent of sports sociology papers have examined youth sports through the eyes of children. Most of what we know involves kids already in the game, and it suggests extrinsic rewards and 'winning' mean far less to them than to adults. In a 2014 George Washington University study, 9 of 10 kids said 'fun' is the main reason they participate. When asked to define fun, they offered up 81 reasons—and ranked 'winning' at No. 48 ."[9]

So let the kids be themselves and have fun, and I guarantee they'll be more focused, improve, and carry over practice skills to game day.

---

9   Aspen Institute Project Play, "The 8 Plays," 2016, accessed February 25, 2019, http://youthreport.projectplay.us/the-8-plays/ask-kids-what-they-want.

KEY COACHING POINTS

- **Keep it light, and have fun while having fun with fundamentals.** You and your players can focus on drills and practice while still enjoying yourselves. Brainstorm ways to have fun that fit with your personality and coaching style.
- **Create an environment that's conducive for kids to relax in and play their best.** Encourage your coaches and the parents to lose their adult shields and have fun with the kids. Don't make it too tense.

COACHING MISTAKES

- **Taking yourself, practices, and games too seriously.** If you press too hard and make the kids tense, the entire experience will become a chore. Leave the negative energy at home.

TRANSFERABLE CAREER SKILL

- **Build camaraderie with coworkers, referral sources, and clients.** Relationships are the backbone of business. Establish a network of people where there's mutual trust and respect and nurture those relationships.
- **Keep it light in the workplace.** A sense of humor and friendliness at the office makes for a happy work culture.

CHAPTER TEN

THE VILLAGE CHIEF'S ROLE (THAT'S YOU!)

I follow three rules: Do the right thing, do the best you can, and always show people you care.

—Lou Holtz

When I first began coaching my softball All-Star team, we knew we had a long way to go and that we needed to focus on the pillars and our fundamentals before we would see any kind of winning results on the scoreboard.

Every season our staff focused on selecting the best group of girls to round out our roster, and every off-season I worked on advancing my coaching skill set. We worked hard at finding new and fun ways to keep the girls interested and improving, as well as gelling even more as a squad.

In the early years, it wasn't uncommon for us to lose games by several runs, even seeing the mercy rules come into effect. Most of the time it didn't bother the girls, though as they got older, they wanted to win. And they kept getting better every year, strengthening their skills in and out of practice.

We'd had a taste (or two) of success over the years, but it wasn't until the last inning of the semifinals of the 2016 Western regional championship tournament that I was able to see how far we'd come. Facing off against an insanely talented Northern California team, we had Graber on the mound. The first batter of the game against us was a girl who came in slightly taller than me. She crushed the very first pitch she saw to the fence, where it was caught by our speedy left fielder, Wheels.

By the last inning, we were up 8–0 because of our incredible team effort and Erin's absolute gem of a game. The emotions finally caught up to me. The game slowed down, and I was able to reflect on the journey this team had taken over the past five years. As I was tearing up, I kept saying to myself, "They did it!" I was so proud of what the "Lovable Losers" had overcome to become the team that was clinching a berth in the championship final. To this day, I can remember that feeling. Even as I wrote this paragraph, I got emotional all over again.

> To get there, we needed the whole village—our coaches, players, and parents—to be part of the program.

To get there, we needed the whole village—our coaches, players, and parents—to be part of the program. Everybody knowing where they fit in and supporting the players every chance they got. I knew that at the end of the day, all that fell on my shoulders to manage. I had to be the decision maker. I had to be in charge, making sure the program was in place and adhered to.

The buck stops with the head coach. There will be tough decisions to make over the course of the season: who plays where; when to call a parent, coach, or kid out on bad behavior; and how the strategy and culture come together. You should consult with your coaches, but all these decisions are your responsibility—the village chief's duty.

It's daunting, sure, but with the program I've detailed in this book, it's navigable. If you don't make those decisions, somebody else will. And that person will no doubt be the loudest in the room and definitely not the one who should be making the tough calls.

It's up to you to lead. You're the one who has to implement the program, bring the team together, and create that environment that will make sure your players are having fun, growing and improving, and giving their focus and energy. You then need to maintain that environment through the end of the season. No one else is going to do it, and it's not going to happen on its own.

Along the way, you'll upset some people as I did when making difficult decisions. The key is to follow the advice from Lou Holtz mentioned at the beginning of this chapter: set expectations and communicate why certain decisions were made. A village chief won't satisfy everybody—and that's okay.

It's inevitable that your decisions and approach will be questioned. Stick with your approach, but be open to feedback. A good village chief is always learning.

Probably ninety-nine times out of one hundred, your season will end with a loss. Unless you're the champion of the league—or states, regionals, or nationals—the final action your players will have on the field or court will be walking off in defeat. For all these losses, you know who will feel that weight the most?

You, that's who. If you're a dedicated coach who's always trying to get better (and if you've read this far, I imagine you are or want to be), there are some losses that will stick with you for weeks, if not until the next season.

In 2014 my U10 Amazing Fireballs soccer team lost a heart-breaker in overtime. It doesn't matter that we were the eighth-ranked team and our opponents were the top seed. I know we could've won that game. Trudging off the field, the teary-eyed girls looked shell shocked but were probably fine by dinnertime. I stewed over that loss for weeks. And it was the same when my Mississauga Tomahawks lacrosse team's season ended with an overtime loss at the provincial championships, when the Raging Unicorns lost in the 12U finals, when the Evil Snowmen lost in the championship game, and when my 2017 14U All-Star team lost to Bonita Valley in the nationals championship game, and on and on.

What else could I have done? How could I have prepared better?

I'll always analyze losses in my head, doing both team reviews and also self-reviews. Should I have pulled that pitcher earlier? Should we have covered that forward differently? And on and on. It's what keeps us striving to get better and learn from our mistakes. After all, we're the village chiefs, and the buck stops with us.

As we come to the end, let's take a step back to look at what we've learned in how to make this all happen, how you can keep improving throughout the season and in the off-season, and how the little things can help give your effort one last push over the hill toward success by discussing the following:

- **your coaches,**
- **your players,**
- **your environment,**

- **your practices and games,**
- **your self-review,**
- **your learning opportunities, and**
- **the little things.**

Your Coaches

It's the beginning of the season. Before you meet your players and establish relationships with them, your first responsibility is assembling the coaching staff and getting buy-in for your strategy and philosophy.

We discussed filling your staff with desirable qualities that you may be lacking (e.g., a walking rule book or a technical expert) and how each coach, like each player, will have a role. In your first meeting with the coaches, make sure they're on board with a team-first environment that allows players (and coaches) to make mistakes and have fun, that they'll be supportive and mean it. There are a lot of coaches whose body language betrays their words. The guy who throws his clipboard and then adds a halfhearted "Okay, great effort!" isn't fooling the kids, who see and internalize his frustration. That won't work on your positive staff.

It's on you to build a relationship with the coaches. When you debrief about practices and games and what you want to accomplish with the kids, also work toward building a personal connection with them. Get to know them, and get them to open up. Doing it over a meal and/or drinks is the best way. By breaking bread and sharing hops, you'll soon have each other's backs and be able to hold each other accountable. You'll be comfortable saying to one another, "That comment you just made to that kid? There's probably a better way of addressing it."

Check in with your coaches throughout the season. Make sure they all stay committed to the program and are evaluating the team's (and their own) performance just as you do. No matter where the coaches are on the playing field, they need to keep their eyes and ears open and work on improving every facet of their skill set. Let the coaches know they should be helping you improve as well if you miss something or slip on any of your commitments.

Your Players

After you've met with the coaches and your team is set, it's up to you to create the first draft of the team identity. What are the strong suits of your players? How are you going to approach games? Establish the team goals with input from the coaches and players. Then as you learn more about each player, you can create individual goals. What is each player going to concentrate on for the coming season, and how do those intentions fit into the team goals? What are their roles, and how will they contribute to the big picture?

Make sure your players are giving their all in each practice and game and that they're bringing a positive attitude and team-first mentality to everything they do. Keep your instructions and direction likewise positive.

Have fun with fundamentals. They can train hard at getting the footwork and placement right and have fun while doing it. Part of the contract with the players is that I expect them to keep on working until they're precise with their movements and execution. And during a drill, if they're not, they know I'll stop and reinforce it. I'll do it with love and a light heart, but I'm still determined to sharpen their skills.

Building a relationship with the kids is just as important as building ones with the coaches. Your one-on-one and group interactions with the kids are what make or break the team. Take the time to get to know your players: what makes them tick and why they're playing. Don't just concentrate on the stars; every single player needs to find a role on the team and feel like part of the bigger picture. Connecting with each of the kids will help you draw them into the team more. Let them know the unwritten contract that comes with being a part of the program: that you expect them to give 100 percent, support each other, work on improving each and every day, and have fun.

Your Environment

With your coaches and players buying into the program, building your team-first culture will be simple as long as you bring the last section of your village—the parents—on board too. They all have rules to buy into as well: positivity and unqualified support at home and in the bleachers. You'll need to be in constant communication with them throughout the entire season. Remind them that their job as parents is to be parents and to let the coaches be the coaches.

The culture you create allows players to thrive by giving them license to be themselves while still being focused on the team and improving their skills with a laser-like focus. As the head coach, you can celebrate each player's individuality through nicknames and finding unique roles for each of them. Celebratory handshakes and rituals such as team chants or synchronized warm-ups all contribute to an environment that highlights positive, supportive attitudes.

At the same time, the atmosphere you're creating is comparable to a pro organization. There's discipline and structure in how your players show up prepared and go about warm-ups, drills, and games. You can still have the expectation that your nine-year-olds will execute certain things with precision: making a catch with their hands correctly aligned, finding their teammate and kicking the ball in front of them to lead them, or executing a bounce pass through two defenders in the key. These things can be accomplished in practice, and if they're not, we'll stop and fix it.

This is also an environment that challenges the kids and supports them when they make mistakes. Your team will mess up in games, but instead of throwing a fit, the coaches, parents, and teammates will be supportive and recognize that mistakes happen. Remind the kids of the importance of mentally checking back into the game and giving their full efforts for the next play. The goal is to learn from those mistakes and get better. Coaches and players expect the most out of each other and take ownership and responsibility. When you set the bar high for yourselves and others, you'll be pleasantly surprised by the results. Be patient and diligent. It can take time to see the results with kids.

Your Practices and Games

Practices are for drills and reps with precision. Games are for letting the kids take control and carry over what's been learned in practice. Maintain that sense of lightness at both—it's serious stuff, but don't heighten the intensity in games just because there's something on the line. You've been practicing hard with the kids all week, expecting the most out of them on drills and scrimmages. Have that same level of expectation, keep the same tone with them come game time, and let them play.

During practices, get the fun with fundamentals down, and make sure they're striving for age-specific precision. Their footwork and motions should be textbook definitions, and if not, stop and reinforce it. And while this is happening, have fun! Keep the jokes going, call out nicknames, exchange barbs with the players and other coaches. Take notes on the drills. What worked? What didn't? Then modify your practices accordingly.

During games, keep the fun intact! Now the kids are in charge, transferring those skills and drills from practice. Your role is on the sidelines. Cheer the team on, and choose when to make your voice heard. Take notes on what you see throughout the game. First are the KPIs you want to track and use for strategy and improvement. How many offensive rebounds did your team grab? How often did your pitcher get ahead of batters? How many quality shots have you taken? How about your opponents?

Also keep track of those cool things you want to point out to the kids after the games. Sure, the long homer and the bicycle kick goal but also the little things that enhance the team-first mentality, such as a high five after a missed shot to support a teammate, keeping their shape, consecutive passes, or your left fielder backing up a play at third. Make sure nobody's left out.

These notes can then inform strategy. The stats you track and moments you observe can give you and the coaching staff items to focus on at the top of the next practice, and the positive takeaways can turn into great team-building feedback (not to mention helmet stickers) for the players. And then it's back to the drills, and rinse and repeat.

Your Seasonal Review

In 2014 baseball superstar Mike Trout led the league in numerous standard offensive statistics including runs, runs batted in, total bases, and extra-base hits along with newer stats such as wins above replacement, runs created, and adjusted batting runs. On the strength of this, he won his first Most Valuable Player award at the ripe old age of twenty-three. In the off-season, Trout became fixated on improving his game, focusing on cutting down his strikeout total—which he did the next year, thus fanning twenty-six fewer times in less games and putting up an arguably better season than the one before.[10]

> Always be
> improving.
> That's what I
> tell players and
> coaches, and
> it's what I tell
> myself.

Always be improving. That's what I tell players and coaches, and it's what I tell myself. At the end of the season, no matter if my team finished in the cellar or walked away with a championship, I study my seasonal notes to see what went right, what went wrong, and what we should be focusing on the next year.

This is the time to look back at your drills and figure out what landed with the kids. You may find that the corner kick move your team worked on relentlessly at practice was a winner because it capitalized on the skills and attributes of your team. You'll also find some plans weren't as effective. Maybe the team didn't end up being as athletic or as fast as you thought; maybe centering the scoring plays around certain kids didn't bear the fruit you'd hoped it would.

It's also the time to look at the stats in total. You may have realizations about how the team performed that didn't dawn on you during the regular season. It sometimes takes that step back to put things in perspective.

---

10   Tyler Kepner, "One Title Mike Trout Hopes to Shed: Strikeout King," New York Times, April 2, 2015, accessed February 27, 2019, https://www.nytimes.com/2015/04/05/sports/baseball/one-title-mike-trout-hopes-to-shed-strikeout-king.html.

My Mimico Mountaineers, the lacrosse team that made their BHAG be to have the best defense in the province, performed well that season, and I was proud of them. At the end of the year, I started digging through the year's stats and found that we had lost a large majority of face-offs in games that mattered. In lacrosse, face-off outcomes are usually around 50 percent. We were losing about 70 percent of them. I didn't realize it was this bad during the season, and staring at the totals, I was blown away. So that off-season, I sat down with Bill, the former star player, and asked for his advice on how to improve our face-off victory rate. Sure enough, we reversed that trend the next year, and our overall game improved even more.

The end of the season is also the time to consider your relationships with the players and coaches. Did all the kids, from stars down to developing players, get their moments to shine? Were their roles clear? Even the nicknames—did everyone have a good one, and were they all feeling like an integral part of the team? These considerations may seem small, but they all contribute to the environment and the kind of team atmosphere you want to have.

Your Learning Opportunities

As my face-off epiphany shows, you can always learn and improve in the off-season. Mike Trout didn't take the winter off after his 2014 MVP season and play video games until spring training, and Nick Saban doesn't vacation for four months once college bowl season is done. There are countless ways to advance your coaching and knowledge. In chapter 3, I talked about various resources, such as clinics and online research. Those aren't just for parents new to the sport. I'm always attune to what workshops are happening nearby, as well as which veteran coaches I can chat with to soak up some knowledge. Even during the writing of this very chapter, I researched how to properly teach sliding to my 10U Thunder Crabs softball team.

That kind of observing and learning should be part of your process throughout the season as well. If your team is up against a superior opponent in basketball, watch how they move the ball up the court, play defense, or execute plays. There might be something in there for you to incorporate with your own kids. When I first began coaching All-Star softball, I knew there would be moments where I would be outcoached. I walked into the opportunity aware of that and looked for lessons. I discovered strategies that I liked from other coaches such as teams playing explosive defense,[11] and there were things that I didn't like, such as players stalling when they were ahead to keep a new inning from starting.

Networking isn't just for your profession. It's for any area of interest you want to excel at. Get out there, and talk shop with people who've been around and have useful tips and techniques. Most opposing coaches will be happy to exchange ideas and advice. The success of your teams and growth of your players doesn't happen by luck. It happens because you make it happen.

A few years ago, I was watching my friend coach her softball team. I was there for moral support and to take notes on areas for improvement. I happened to be sitting next to her husband, a buddy of mine in his own right. This guy wasn't a coach, and while he was a casual fan, he wasn't a huge aficionado of the game. As we were watching, he kept name-dropping people he knew who were "really knowledgeable" about softball, folks who really knew their stuff.

I nodded and smiled and kept watching the game unfold. My buddy started asking questions about plays on the field. Why would

---

11   Thank you, Scott Cox and the incredible team of girls from La Cañada!

we do that? Why's the runner going back? And on and on. I answered each and every one of his questions calmly. After about ten of these exchanges, he looked at me and said, "Steve, how the heck do you know all this?"

I briefly wondered if he thought our success was dumb luck and then responded, "Well, I work every day to learn this game at the highest level. I put together a great coaching staff who knows their stuff, and we're constantly studying and improving. We take this seriously behind the scenes." I think he got the message.

It's true. It's not enough to be a former athlete who excelled at the sport. And it's not enough to be a parent who's just enthusiastic about the position. No matter what you're coaching, just like the kids whose experience is in your hands, you have to take it seriously and have fun doing it.

The Little Things

Throughout this book, I've at times focused on components that may have seemed trivial. The design of your team logo and wearing uniforms. Nicknames. Making sure your players' bags are neatly organized. Getting every player her or his moment to shine. Letting the kids shout out the great plays they noticed during the game.

They may seem like small potatoes, but what they're doing is giving the kids autonomy and responsibility and making them feel like part of a united team that's operating like a professional organization. It's giving them a sense of pride in showing up to practices and games and a sense of belonging to a thing bigger than themselves.

My 10U Thunder Crabs softball team strode onto the field for opening day with all except one practice canceled due to bad weather. We were behind on every drill and fundamental I wanted to begin instilling in the kids. However, just like the Blue Dolphins, Purple Penguins, Path of Destruction, Punching Pandas, Ninja Nightcrawlers, Junkyard Bunnies, and Emus before them, when we got onto the diamond, we had two ingredients that gave a sense of confidence and unity to our girls. One, swagger: we were professional and organized in the way we set up our bags, mitts, bats, and helmets. Two, swag: in the fifty-degree weather, our players were dressed in our Thunder Crab gear, which included matching sweatshirts, pants, and socks. It wasn't just the opposing players who were dumbstruck. Over the course of the day, I had four coaches ask me where we got our clothing and how we looked so good.

Making sure each player has a role and gets those moments may sound like a little thing to a lot of teams. There are some coaches who when faced with a player who doesn't have an advanced skill set on the field, will just look for a place to hide them where they'll do the least amount of damage.

Finding a place and role for your developing players isn't a small thing. It's part of the program that makes sure that every kid is contributing to the team, giving it their all, and having fun. There's a good chance that those developing players are the ones for whom the special moments and team unity will mean the most and create the most lasting memories.

I began this book saying that while my teams and players have won championships large and small, have proven themselves with excellent play and improvement on the fields and courts, and gone on to be successful teenage athletes, my favorite moments sometimes have nothing to do with the final score or athletic prowess.

Thirty years ago, in my early days with youth sports, I was coaching middle-school-aged kids in basketball in my hometown of Midland, Ontario, and it was the last day of a well-run season. We were in the final minutes of this final game when I noticed that the opponents had put an undersized kid on the floor who I knew hadn't made a basket the entire year. I pulled my point guard aside and said, "Hey, that kid hasn't scored the entire season."

I didn't have to say anything else. "I'm on it, Coach," replied my guard. Quicker than you can say Spud Webb, he caught an inbound pass and dribbled right up to the small, unlucky kid, basically handing him a steal. The kid grabbed it and went up for a shot … but the ball clanked off the rim. Without missing a beat, one of my other players, attuned to what was happening, subtly batted the rebound right back toward the kid. This time he put it up, and it went in for his first two points of the season.

The gym—both sides and both teams—erupted in joy. There's no doubt in my mind that this would be a viral video had it not been the pre-YouTube days of the early 1990s. This is a huge part of what the program is: developing not just players but also good sports, competitors, and people. It was a standout memory of my coaching career.

After a full season of incorporating the lessons from these chapters—building your team; getting everyone on the same page; establishing a supportive, team-first, fun environment; running meticulous practices; overseeing kid-controlled games; and paying attention to all the little things—take a moment to enjoy what you've created and how far your group of individuals have come, together.

As I was writing this book, our 2019 10U All-Star softball team wrapped up its season with a heartbreaking extra inning 2–1 defeat, giving me that moment to enjoy what we'd created. I couldn't have been prouder of the team. Though we had lost, we'd played as close to mistake-free softball as possible. We had plenty of ups and downs throughout the season but ended on a high note, playing with incredible skill, precision, and emotion and leaving it all on the field.

Maybe the girls weren't able to put things in perspective with that sting of a close loss, but I sat back the entire game and took it all in. I cherished AK's perfect "sneaky" bunt, Marilyn's command behind the plate, Swartzy and Peyton's critical infield plays, Breezy's mastery of the outfield, and Dani's almost perfectly pitched game, methodically frustrating a team that averaged over ten runs a game. Each player embraced her role, and we competed with the team that went on to win the 2019 Western nationals championship. It took the entire village of players, coaches, and parents to accomplish this, and the results were amazing.

When you get that opportunity to take it all in, be proud of the impact you've made. It may be for that brief moment of time called a season, or it could be much more than that. It could be a memory the players, coaches, and parents take with them for years to come. Whether your year ends with a win or a loss, it won't matter. You've created success all season and an incredible experience for your entire village … but most importantly, for the kids. And that's the real reason we do it.

KEY COACHING POINTS

- **The buck stops with you.** You're the village chief, and you need to take control. There will be important decisions throughout your season, from game strategies such as pulling a pitcher to larger decisions such as crafting your team identity, and it's your job to make them. Take advice from others, but ultimately, you're in charge of the team and making the program happen.

- **Enjoy yourself.** Like the kids, you wouldn't be here if you didn't have fun doing it in the first place. Take your practices and games seriously, and never forget why you're there and how to enjoy it.

COACHING MISTAKES

- **Being a passive leader.** If you don't show decisiveness and clarity of thought, others will take advantage of you. Loud parents, undisciplined kids, and aggressive coaches can have their worst instincts bolstered if there's not strength up top.

TRANSFERABLE CAREER SKILL

- Whether you're the CEO, manager, analyst, or any other title, **you're in control of certain aspects of your job.** Take responsibility, and hold yourself accountable for those decisions.

ACKNOWLEDGMENTS

MY FAMILY ...

First and foremost, my family. Esther, Krista, and Tyler have supported me throughout this entire process of coaching through writing this book; they have been understanding and supportive every step of the way. They all sacrificed for the greater good of the teams and kids that I coached over the years. They shared their dad and husband with hundreds of other kids and parents.

Krista and Tyler, you were the reason that I got deeply involved in coaching again and you both are the inspiration for this book. I am so grateful I had the opportunity to coach both of you for as long as I did. I had such an amazing time coaching you and watching you grow up so quickly on and off the field. Love, Dad!

In both cases, the last game I ever coached them ended in a tough loss. Krista's El Segundo Eagles 14U softball team lost in the Western nationals championship game and Tyler's Raging Unicorns U12 soccer team lost in the league tournament championship game. I had a strong feeling that each of those games were probably the last for my days of coaching them. I was able to enjoy the moments of the games, working closely with them and, as their coach and parent, seeing them having fun playing a sport with their teammates and performing at a high level. I was so proud walking off the field knowing that we ended things on a very positive note.

Behind many great coaches are the amazing supportive spouses. Esther's input has been invaluable and I would not have had the success I did without her.

Esther, you didn't always agree with my decisions on and off the field (coaching a team of ten-year-olds without Krista or Tyler on the team was a bit of a doozy), but your loyalty, input, and support was one of my secrets to success. You constantly challenge me to be a better husband, father, and coach, and I am forever grateful to have such an incredible partner and friend.

I was the second of five kids (Belynda, me, Laura, Joanna, and Jamie) in our family and that taught me a lot about relationships, sharing, and how to eat fast so you can get first shot at any leftovers! After my parents divorced, my mom (Paula Baldwin) did her best to keep us all in line, but she was severely outnumbered. My older sister, Belynda Kerelchuk, stepped up for me in a way that she probably doesn't remember, nor will she ever understand the impact she had on my life.

Belynda, you helped guide me through some of the tougher years growing up. I was a lost and often confused kid and you helped keep me on the right path. I would not have had the success I have had in my life without your guidance and support.

THE COACHES THAT INSPIRED ME AS A PLAYER ...

My first coach, who also happened to be my dad, Len Cleland. My dad showed me a glimpse of what I wanted to do later in life. His teams were always well prepared and competitive, yet he had a fun tone and he acted goofy with his players. He seemed to have so much fun coaching my teams and then coaching against me for a rival elementary school where he taught the eighth grade. The kids loved playing for him. Whether it was kids that he taught or kids that he coached, he made an impact on many of them.

Dad, thanks for coaching me and giving me the basic framework of a great coach!

Harry Chaddington, who coached me in several sports in elementary school. I remember the time he sat me down after a tough loss in a tournament championship game. I was upset because I played really hard and we lost. Even more upsetting to me was that we didn't get trophies for second place. Harry got a little heated and took that opportunity for the next three to five minutes to explain to me how meaningless trophies were. I can still hear his voice in the dressing room telling me to stop acting like a baby and to focus on what was really important ... the team, the improvement we had shown (nobody expected us in the finals), and the fun we had accomplishing what we did. He finished by commenting that my behavior was not a good example for the other players and he expected better leadership from his star player. He was right and over thirty-five years later, I still remember that moment like it was yesterday. Thanks Harry!

My high school basketball coach, Jeff Attwood. You knew he cared about you not only as a player but as a developing human being. He was a great role model for me in my critical high school years. I adopted many aspects of Mr. Attwood's coaching style into mine. Thirty years later, I have even found myself saying in some tough game situations, "How would Mr. Attwood react?" That is impact!

Jeff, you had a huge impact on my style and thought process in coaching. I always appreciated your calm-under-pressure style and the way you treated me and my teammates in a positive way.

Hall of Fame lacrosse coach Jim Bishop. I only had two hours with him at a coaching clinic, but he drilled into me the importance of the basic fundamentals and how mastering them will make or break your teams. His advice became my first pillar of coaching. One of the main underlying foundations of every single team I ever coached.

I played a lot of sports over the years so there were many other coaches who had an impact on me as a player and as a coach. Whether it was a positive interaction or a behavior that taught me something that I did not want to model, I formed my early coaching style by borrowing from the many who volunteered their time to coach me and my teammates. I am very grateful for the significant impact they all had in my life.

THE COACHES WHOM I COACHED WITH AND AGAINST ...

Rob Graner had a big impact on me over the past decade. We were an awesome team together because we complemented each other so well. With two older boys, Rob's experience and approach to coaching the kids and working with the parents was extremely helpful in navigating the many seasons we coached together. It all started with the Green Grasshoppers and the postseason party. After a few beers, we made a commitment to keep our group of girls together and teach them about life through sport for as long as we could. We didn't always see things the same and there were plenty of challenges along the way, but we did exactly what we set out to do and I am glad we finished that part of my coaching journey together.

Rob, we had the vision and we created an environment that led to magic on the field. You believed in me and my approach with the kids and you were always there to support me and help me further develop technical, strategic, and political aspects of coaching. Thank you for being a great mentor.

When I coached the 2019 10U all-star team without Rob, I could still hear his voice in my ear.

I can't name all the coaches, but so many helped me through the highs and lows season after season. Brad Wadge, Rick Mack, Lance Ralls, Tony Temblador, Brad Swartzlander, Steve Hopkins, and Scott Cox all impacted me at some point in my coaching journey.

There are so many more. Many of the coaches I worked with helped me become the coach that I am today. Each one of them was unique, bringing something to the table that I was able to learn from. I have been so fortunate in my coaching career to have worked with and against so many talented coaches.

OTHER LEADERS ...

The incredible leaders that took time out of their busy schedules to discuss the concepts of the book and how it might impact coaches and, ultimately, the kids. I spent a lot of time talking about leadership, coaching ideas and principles, marketing and branding, etc. with Lance Giroux, Chris Keldorf, Ben Watkins, Dan Owen, Ocean Fine (who came up with the title "The Village Chief" after a long night of wine drinking and discussing the book), Drew Boyles, David Anderson, Jamie Douraghy, Paul Olshan, and John Bly to name a few.

My forum group in Entrepreneurs' Organization: John Koudsi, Randy Horn, Matt Casden, Mitch Langstein, Mike Murphy, and Brent Whitfield. These guys helped me from the time the book was just an idea through today. I am so fortunate to have a group like this that inspires me, pushes me, and supports me.

THE KIDS ...

Finally, the players. The hundreds of kids that I have coached over the past thirty years. When I think about some of the best moments of my coaching career, it is not just the championships, wins, and triumphs that make me most proud. It is the journey I took with these kids. I think about Aiden Pagel's first hit and his slide at home, the smile on his face and the even bigger smile on his dad Larry's face. I think about that magical night where Jura Glennie hit the game-winning double (her first hit of the season) in the last inning of the championship game for the Junkyard Bunnies, capping off a huge comeback win. Most of the crowd figured that this at-bat was going to be her forty-sixth strike-out of the season, but Jura got her first hit and became a hero in that one moment! I think about Cullen Foote, the McCrae twins, and Jay Preece from the Mimico Mountaineer seasons, where they turned into young men as we toured all over Ontario. The kids from the Flying Monkeys, Swamp Donkeys, Raging Unicorns, Fire-Breathing Rubber Duckies, Mitey Moose Mashers, Evil Snowmen, Thunder Chickens, the Flamethrowers (the greatest 0-11 hockey team of all time), and the list goes on and on. I think about the hotel stays, bonding with teammates between games, curfew police, breaking up elevator tag, the late-night coaching meetings, the early morning wake-up calls, the games under the lights, the games in the pouring rain, dancing competitions during a rain delay, team dinners, and the games in the 110-degree heat. The kids made me laugh and cry, they disappointed me, they frustrated me, and sometimes they made me sad. They put me through every emotion imaginable, but most of all they made me proud. My coaching journey has been awesome and so rewarding for me personally because of the kids that I get the opportunity to coach.

The kids are the real reason I wrote this book. I have seen kids flourish in the system described in this book, and it makes all the difference in the world to them, the team, and their parents. I hope that, over the long term, some of those kids will think of me and how I may have impacted their life. There may be one moment where I may have positively impacted a kid's life permanently. How cool is that?

ABOUT THE AUTHOR

Steve Cleland is a seasoned entrepreneur, certified public accountant (CPA), certified fraud examiner (CFE), and sought-after speaker. Steve's greatest passion is coaching sports. Steve has been coaching recreational, All-Star, club, travel, and rep teams in several sports over the last thirty years. In the last decade alone, Steve coached over five hundred kids on more than fifty teams in several sports, ran 1,250+ practices, and coached over eight hundred games.

Blending the business/entrepreneurial world with his extensive on-field experience, Steve has mastered creating an environment for success where kids, parents, and coaches thrive. Steve firmly believes that success in youth sports is about more than winning a game or a championship: it's about maximizing the potential of every player, parent, and coach on your team; kids having fun playing a sport with their friends; and developing a sense of selflessness, grit, confidence, and respect for the game, teammates, and opponents.

Steve is now sharing his approach and his experiences, as well as the successes, setbacks, failures, and the related lessons learned along the way. Steve's mission is to positively impact as many kids' lives as possible ... one coach at a time.

MORE FROM COACH STEVE CLELAND

Go to www.SteveCleland.com for additional coaching resources and to learn more about Steve as an entrepreneur, speaker, CPA, CFE, and coach.

CPSIA information can be obtained
at www.ICGtesting.com
Printed in the USA
LVHW021636180220
647330LV00011B/778